What people are saying about
Foundations of Children's Evangelism . . .

"Dick is a legendary figure in kids ministry. His pioneering spirit and passionate heart have made an indelible imprint on the church in America and around the world. Dick's ministry will leave a lasting legacy because he is determined to equip those around him with better tools and resources than he had when he began in ministry. And that is why you *need* this book! Dick has packed decades of kids ministry wisdom into one resource! It will change your ministry—big time!"

—**Brian Dollar**, creator of High Voltage Kids Ministry Resources, author of *I Blew It!* and *Talk Now and Later*, associate and kids pastor at First Assembly of God, North Little Rock, AR

"I have seen a lot of trends come and go in children's ministry over the past four decades, yet for over four decades I have seen my friend Dick Gruber focus on the main thing, which is evangelizing kids and giving them the gospel. One of the first people I ever called with a question about children's ministry was Dick Gruber. Dick has always been free to share whatever he knows to whoever wants to learn. This book will help you get focused, stay focused, and be focused on what really matters in children's ministry—reaching and discipling kids!"

—**Jim Wideman**, children's ministry pioneer, author, and leadership coach, Jimwideman.com

"Where did kids ministry originate? I'm not sure, but I'm confident that Dick Gruber must have been there. He has more than forty years of ministry experience in many contexts: children's pastor in small and large churches, university children's ministries specialist, speaker, and writer. Dick has spoken at our camps and training events all across our network for the fifteen years that I have served as Christian education director. His material is practical and Bible based. You can read any of his material and be confident that it will be well worth the read and investment of your time."

—**Wayne Rimmer**, Christian education/children's ministry director, Potomac Ministry Network of the Assemblies of God

"Dick Gruber is constantly my greatest source of inspiration and foundation in ministering to kids. His methods are grounded in the Bible, tested in the real world, and flowing with creativity. His mission field for over forty years has been the hearts of children, and he has the stories and the wisdom to show for it! Besides being an encourager and mentor, he's a great dad and an awesome grandfather to my kids—it doesn't get any better than that!"

—**Aaron Gruber**, lead kids pastor, Emmanuel Christian Center, Spring Lake Park, MN

"Dick Gruber's forty-plus years of loving Jesus and loving children combine in this benchmark work. Be informed and be inspired by his reflections, gleaned from a lifetime of service to God's kids."

—**Rob Evans**, www.donutman.streamlinenettrial.co.uk

"Dick Gruber's many years of experience will provide helpful insights for anyone desiring to expand their understanding of children's ministry."

—**Steve Adams**, children's pastor, Saddleback Church, Lake Forest, CA

"Dr. Dick Gruber's take on evangelizing kids has to be the most promising work on the subject in years because, if for no other reason, his experience in this realm is vast. Since Bible college, I have seen him lead children to the Savior through local church ministries, Christian summer camps, and evangelistic rallies of all descriptions. In addition, Dick has been an in-demand speaker on children's ministry around the world for decades. As a communicator he is captivating because he is just as focused on his listeners as he is on his message, and that is just one of the secrets to his success. Only eternity will tell of the impact his ministry has had on the countless boys and girls he has led to Christ and, beyond that, his influence through all those he has trained. One last word that must be said about Professor Gruber is the fact that, in spite of his talents and achievements, he is a humble servant of God with whom anyone can relate, if not count as a friend."

—**Bob Hahn**, lead pastor, Peace Chapel, Morris, IL

"I have had the pleasure of working with Dick Gruber in countless children's summer camps and kids ministry trainings, and have observed him teaching children's ministry students in the university setting. Dick has a unique gift of communicating the good news to children in a way that is not only easily understood, but also prompts a positive response. Dick teaches more than methods; he teaches us how to partner with the power of the Holy Spirit to reach children."

—**George Krebs**, Christian education director, Pen/Del Ministry Network of the Assemblies of God

FOUNDATIONS OF CHILDREN'S EVANGELISM

How to Lead Kids to Christ

LOGION® PRESS

FOUNDATIONS OF CHILDREN'S EVANGELISM

*How to Lead
Kids to
Christ*

DICK GRUBER, DMin

Published by Logion Press
1445 N. Boonville Ave.
Springfield, Missouri 65802
www.myhealthychurch.com

Cover and interior design and formatting by Livingstone Corporation (www.livingstonecorp.com)

ISBN: 978-1-60731-478-3

Printed in the United States of America

21 20 19 18 17 • 1 2 3 4 5

CONTENTS

PREFACE

The term "soul winning" was commonly used when I came to Christ and began helping in children's ministries in the mid-1970s. It wasn't unusual back then for a children's leader to exclaim, "We won five kids to Christ," or, "We just won three children in an evangelist outreach." I even attended a conference entitled, "Win a Child." Being literally minded, I wondered how many children would be given away as door prizes that week.

Terminology has morphed as much as methodology since the 7'0s. Now instead of "win," we say reach. Instead of "Kid's Crusade," we say, "Family Fun Fest," or "Super Saturday." In years past, it was a common practice of churches to host annual Kid's Crusades and vacation Bible school each summer. Children's leaders were taught in workshops and at conventions to allow time for children to respond to the Gospel in every class and club meeting.

I witnessed this firsthand as I sat in the back of children's church my first Sunday in a local evangelical church. After a variety-packed presentation of a singular theme, the woman leading the children's church time encouraged boys and girls to respond to Christ and trust Him for their salvation. I was amazed and blessed by this experience. I knew in my heart that I must be allowed to participate in reaching children.

I've watched methods constantly evolve to meet the current cultural needs, while the commission to reach boys and girls remains constant. God loves children. Jim Wideman writes, "Loving people, creating memories for families, and tying those memories to the person of Jesus and His example are what the church should be about."[1]

This is a book about loving and creating memories for children. It's about sharing the Gospel of Jesus Christ with boys and girls. It has been my privilege as a children's leader to present the gospel and pray with children to come to Christ. My greatest joy has been to pray with my own children as they put their faith and trust in Jesus. My oldest, Sarah, was just four years old when she questioned, "Dad, can I have Jesus in my heart?" I knew that at four, she didn't understand the full implications of what she was asking. That didn't stop us from praying together. That night, I explained salvation in terms she would understand, then Sarah and I prayed. She made her first step towards a life of discipleship with Christ.

My desire is that you will experience similar joy. In those days I hadn't yet considered a Biblical theology of evangelizing children. I knew nothing of questions surrounding an age of accountability, or why a church should engage in reaching kids. I did know that I loved Jesus and wanted to share His life with children and their families. My heart for the evangelism of children is, I believe, a reflection of God's heart for His little ones. Jesus loves the little children. It's more than a song; it's a fact. It is with this heart that I began research and writing in the early 2000s.

---

1   Jim Wideman, *Tweetable Leadership* (Murfreesboro, TN: 2015), 116.

This book begins with a presentation of research and grows into practical application of that study. The following pages contain a collection of writings based in study of God's Word, research in a Christian college library, and practical experience gained reaching children through a variety of outreach venues.

I trust that the serious student of the evangelism of children will find ideas, theology, and resources to support his/her dedication to this important global task. Consider this work as a launching pad into your own research and experience as you reach the children for Jesus.

This book is divided into two sections: Section One—Research and Writings, and Section Two—Practical Ideas for Evangelizing Children.

The first section provides you with a biblical theology of the evangelism of children, a summary of research into past and current writings on this topic, a response to these topics, and ethical considerations when giving altar calls to children. The student of ministry to children must remember to lay every brick of evangelism on a solid foundation of God's great love for children. Writers through the ages have recognized this and written about with passion. I pray that the quotes contained in this work will help you to better articulate your passion for children.

Section Two gives you a study on prayer for the children's leader, ways to promote your ministry, developing outreach events, and how to lead a child to Christ. This section is not all-inclusive. I am certain that there are other topics in evangelism of children that could have been covered. There is intentionality in my leaving out specific programs like vacation Bible school. Evangelistic programs come and go.

Over time, I have seen fads in evangelism fade, while basic principles remain constant. Examples of specific current programs and outreach events can be accessed online. Throughout your life and ministry, you will present outreach events or programs in your church and community. Ideas for these may come through reading, networking with other children's leaders, or a passing comment made at a national conference. Some of your events will be incredibly successful. Others will not. Don't give up.

For three years I served at a church and had incredible success reaching kids through side-yard parties in local neighborhoods. Clowns, puppets, stories, songs, and prizes were presented and children as well as parents came to know Christ. I then moved to a new ministry in a church in another state. There, my neighborhood outreach failed in an epic way. I was determined to discover what evangelistic method(s) would work in the culture of that church and community. After a bit of trial and error, I was reaching children in that new place. Every church is different. Every community is different. I trust that after reading this book, you will step out and reach children in a way that complements your church's ministry in the community.

Evangelism of children should never be allowed to sit gathering mold in the children's department storage room. The call to evangelize boys and girls is given to the entire church. The children's leader must seek ways to mobilize today's church to reach the next generation. These ways should be in keeping with the church culture and vision of your lead pastor. Lynda Freeman pens, "Before you can begin to design your unique recipe for children's ministry, you need to understand your own church's history, community, and culture."[2]

There are many parents, leaders, and teenagers who have inspired me over the years to do more in reaching children. I thank God for you. Those who've led, helped, and served in classes, clubs, and special events set a high standard for me with their preparation, passion, and pursuit of God's best for His children. Their dedication to evangelizing children has pushed me to do more, grow in my vision, and eventually write this book.

2   Lynda Freeman, "No Cookie-Cutter Children's Ministries," *Pulse: Pumping Life into Your Kids Ministry*, ed. Ryan and Beth Frank (KidzMatter Inc., 2014).

CHAPTER 1

INTRODUCTION

The term "evangelizing children" carries with it many preconceptions, both positive and negative. On the positive side we find Jesus welcoming and blessing children in Matthew 19. He establishes a pattern for reaching children by His words and deeds. Of this encounter Edward Hayes wrote, "To Him, the recovery of one lost child was top priority."[1]

Throughout the years well-meaning ministers have interpreted and acted upon the example of Christ. Some have approached children with the love of Christ, presenting His message with care while utilizing appropriate methodology. Others have emotionally and verbally abused, scared, or offended little ones based on personal paradigms that are less than child-friendly. Although Jonathan Edwards preached of God's love and care for children, he also presented the full wrath of an angry God to boys and girls. Catherine Brekus writes of this Great Awakening preacher, "To make children see their unworthiness, Edwards did not hesitate to use fear."[2] Edwards had no background in

---

1 Edward L Hayes, "Evangelism of Children," *Bibliotheca sacra* 132, no. 527 (July–September 1975): 250–264.
2 Catherine A. Brekus, "Children of Wrath, Children of Grace: Jonathan Edwards and the

modern psychology, as its rise happened more than a century after his ministry. It would seem that he just knew how to exploit common childhood fears when preaching to children.[3]

Some of today's children's leaders continue in the tradition of fear and manipulative crowd psychology. These should pay attention to the warning of Matthew 18:6, "If anyone causes one of these little ones—those who believe in me—to stumble, it would be better for them to have a large millstone hung around their neck and to be drowned in the depths of the sea."

Regardless of approach, the evangelism of children is, and will continue to be, an important aspect of Christian ministry. The leader of the contemporary church should not ignore this. He should rather strive to embrace the concept of evangelizing children, discovering new methods in reaching each new generation.

This writing will address the following assertions: There is a biblical mandate to evangelize children. This mandate requires a historical and programmatic response on the part of the contemporary Christian church.

These statements bring several questions to mind, the foremost of which is, "What does the Bible say about reaching children?" Others that must be considered include, "Can children be lost? Can they be saved? Can a child understand salvation? What is the church's response to the biblical mandate? Should the church approach children holistically when presenting the gospel?" This work will endeavor to answer these and other questions which arise when one studies children and salvation from biblical, historical, and social perspectives.

Perhaps you, the reader, have approached children and min-

Puritan Culture of Child Rearing" in *The Child in Christian Thought* (Grand Rapids: William Eerdmans Publishing Company, 2001), 315.

3   Ibid., 316.

istry to them in the way that George Barna describes in his 2001 book, *Transforming Children into Spiritual Champions.* Concerning children, Barna writes, "In my mind, they were people en route to significance—i.e., adulthood—but were not yet deserving of the choice resources."[4] Barna goes on to describe how, based on solid research into children's ministry, he was compelled to reconsider his and the church's roles in reaching children.

A threefold biblical mandate will be presented in this work. It encompasses inclusion, invitation, and instruction. The reader will see that these areas are given reoccurring emphasis in the Old and New Testaments. The historical literature review beginning with the early church and progressing until now will help unpack these perspectives. The reader will find in reading this that stirring philosophical arguments for evangelizing children will be presented.

Upon reading this, one must, like George Barna, reconsider his and the church's roles in recognizing the significance of evangelizing children, the position of children in the body of Christ, and their place in the life of the Church.

Confronting the Age of Accountability

One cannot begin a study on evangelizing children without first addressing the age of accountability. "It cannot be denied that children sin (Gen. 8:21); that is evident empirically as well as theologically!"[5] For years, church leaders have attempted to define an age at which a child can be held accountable for her sinful actions. Some have established a specific age, while others have rejected the concept altogether.

---

4 George Barna, *Transforming Children into Spiritual Champions* (Ventura: Regal Books, 2003), 11.

5 Scottie May, Beth Poterski, Catherine Stonehouse, and Linda Cannell, *Children Matter* (Grand Rapids: William Eerdmans Publishing, 2005), 51.

Considering a possible "age of accountability" will inform your approach to evangelizing boys and girls. Your belief concerning this age of accountability will help determine your target audience when running outreach events. It will give you direction for the acceptance of the child convert. This is not an exhaustive study on the age of accountability,[6] but rather a discussion starter that you can step in and out of as you begin to think about the child as a sinner who can be saved by grace.

Augustine taught that children begin life in a state of "non-innocence."[7] Children basically do not sin until they have the physical strength and language skills to do so. Once they have attained these, they will sin. Other writers of the fourth century and beyond lay the burden of original sin on the children. It is common today among evangelicals to believe that, born with it or not, children do sin and are in need of a Savior. Edward Hammond wrote in his 1878 book entitled *The Conversion of Children*, "All Christians of every name agree that 'the wages of sin is death,' and it must be admitted that, at as early an age as a child is capable of knowing right from wrong, it is capable of sinning."[8]

---

6   The age of accountability question will be more fully discussed in the chapter entitled, "Ethical Considerations When Giving Altar Calls to Children."

7   Mary Ellen Stortz, "Where or When Was Your Servant Innocent? Augustine on Childhood" in *The Child in Christian Thought* (Grand Rapids: William Eerdmans Publishing Company, 2001), 82, 85. "Between innocence and depravity Augustine posed a third possibility: non-innocence. Any innocence in childhood resided in physical weakness—that is, in being unable to harm anyone else *(In-nocens*, literally not harming)." Augustine's views are further explained as the author writes, "The meaning of accountability shifted throughout these three initial stages of the life cycle. While the infant's non-innocence might be judged pre-moral due to its lack of physical strength, the child's developing language skills conferred both an ability to communicate and increasing accountability for behavior. A child was held accountable if he or she violated a verbal rule—often an arbitrary one. Adolescence heralded the emergence of reason, and a youth faced even greater accountability for his or her behavior."

8   Edward Payson Hammond, *The Conversion of Children* (New York: N. Tibbals and Sons, 1878), 5. "All Christians of every name agree that 'the wages of sin is death,' and it must be admitted that, at as early an age as a child is capable of knowing right from

This is further emphasized by Assemblies of God Pastor Richard Dresselhaus as he writes, "Only through a careful teaching of the Word of God, and as the Spirit is active, will these children recognize their need and feel drawn by the Spirit to salvation."[9] Based on the assumption that all children sin, the church has sought throughout the ages to establish an age at which the child is accountable for that sin. Once accountability is established, then the child can be brought into salvation through Jesus.[10]

Although Scripture does not give such an age, many have attempted to describe it. Sam Doherty, who has served with Child Evangelism Fellowship in Ireland and Europe for over fifty years, writes, "The Bible does not give an age, and neither should we. Children differ from each other. But the Lord Jesus did speak about little ones trusting him (Matthew 18:6)."[11] It is evident after study of available historic literature that an age of accountability is not taught in the Scriptures. The basis for it can be logically deduced.[12] One can appreciate Pastor Dresselhaus's writing concerning the age of accountability. His book, *Teaching for Decision*, was a mainstay for Sunday school teacher training in the 1970s and '80s. Dresselhaus pens, "Obviously, it is impossible to determine a uniform age when all children reach this point of awareness."[13]

---

wrong, it is capable of sinning. To defer the capacity for conversion to a more mature age than this, would be to leave to everlasting destruction all children past the age of sinning who die while they are too young to be converted. Marvel not that we say a young child can be born again, for, as even a little child bitten by the serpents in the wilderness was capable of looking upon the brazen serpent, so the youngest can now look unto Jesus and be saved."

9 Richard L. Dresselhaus, *Teaching for Decision* (Springfield: Gospel Publishing House, 1973), 56.

10 See Chapter 5, "Ethical Considerations When Giving Altar Calls to Children."

11 Sam Doherty, *How to Evangelize Children* (Northern Ireland: CEF Specialized Book Ministry, 2003), 12.

12 Hayes, "Evangelism of Children," 254.

13 Dresselhaus, *Teaching for Decision*, 57. "The rate of growth and maturity varies radically, according to ability and background. Some children have a basic comprehension of

The age of accountability question may never be fully answered on planet earth. When is a child old enough to understand? How do you approach salvation when you feel he is ready? Is the church guilty of pushing for salvation commitments at too early an age? Daniel Smith wrote in 1987,

> Some argue that young children are not able to understand the issues of faith and grace. I realize that children mature at different rates, and the ability to discern spiritual issues comes at a different point for different individuals. However, many have understood salvation by grace through faith at a very early age. We should present a consistent gospel message even to young children.[14]

In 1970, William Hendricks, Baptist theologian, further explains why the church must present the gospel to children. He talks of a "moment" when the child awakens to the spiritual truth of salvation and thus accountability.[15]

Church leaders and teachers who spend at the most two to three hours a week with children can hardly be expected to know a child well enough to estimate his readiness to receive Christ. So the children's leader must do as Lois Lebar encouraged in her 1952 book, *Children in the Bible School*. Ms. Lebar implores the leader to "provide frequent opportunities to say yes

---

the gospel at age four or five. Others may reach the age of 10 before they seem ready to grasp the message of the gospel. At any rate, salvation is conditioned upon some ability to understand the basic plan of salvation. This is true for children as well as adults."

14 Daniel H. Smith, *How to Lead a Child to Christ* (Chicago: Moody Press, 1987), 15.

15 William Hendricks, "The Age of Accountability," in *Children and Conversion,* ed. by Clifford Ingle (Nashville: Broadman Press, 1970), 84, 97. "The time of accountability is the moment of grace when one is brought to a decision for or against Christ by the Spirit. This moment requires the proclamation of the Word, the drawing of the Spirit, and the yielding of the individual to God. Until this moment is possible, one may leave children in the hands of God. Evidences are that we are holding very young children accountable for too much and not holding adults, who have professed Christ, accountable for enough."

to Christ."[16] The task of the church, then, is to regularly provide opportunities for children to be challenged at their varying levels of understanding to make a conscious decision for Christ.

Concerns over the age of accountability often arise when the children's leader or pastor is confronted with the question, "What if the child were to die?" A fear of impending doom then motivates the leader to evangelize the child. Several writers have adopted a reverse approach. It is based on the assumption that a sufficient Christian theology for the evangelism and discipleship of children must be based on the supposition that children will live. Children must be taught of their importance in God's eternal scheme rather than be frightened by impending death.[17] An invitation to receive abundant life in Jesus is a much worthier motivation than providing an eternal fire escape.

When incorporating boys and girls into the faith community, the motivation of insuring that children have a new life in Jesus must supersede any other. God is just and loves the children. Edward Hayes wrote, "God stands ready to save the child on the exercise of the child's faith. If the child is a five-year-old, God will be pleased to accept a five-year-old response. If the child is ten, then God will accept a ten-year-old faith response."[18]

The task of the would-be leader may not be that of discerning the age of accountability, but rather advancing the gospel to children of all ages utilizing appropriate methodology

---

16 Lois E. Lebar, *Children in the Bible School* (Old Tappan, NJ: Fleming H. Revell Company, 1952), 171. "If we provide small children frequent opportunities to say, 'yes' to Christ in accordance with their limited comprehension of Him, we shall never err by hindering them from coming to the Savior, nor by being responsible for their making a mere profession before the Spirit has prepared the heart. We shall never be guilty of going to either extreme if we give our groups of children numerous occasions to confess their love of Christ, and then deal individually with those who seek salvation, a miracle which happens once for all time and eternity."

17 William L. Hendricks, *A Theology for Children* (Nashville: Broadman Press, 1980), 17.

18 Hayes, "Evangelism of Children," 261.

backed with the pure motive of God's love. The task of this writing is not to devise or discern, nor answer or solve, the dilemma of the age of accountability. The age of accountability is a topic that will be the subject of continuing debate long after this work is complete. The purpose of this thesis is to demonstrate a biblical mandate for advancing the gospel to children young and old. This advancement must move forward utilizing appropriate methodology applied out of a motivation to share God's love.

Why Should We Evangelize Children?

In the book *Children in the Bible School*, Lois Lebar answers the question, "Why bring the gospel to children?"[19] Ms. Lebar provides eight reasons. I've borrowed two of her answers and added a third of my own. These best represent today's reasons for reaching children. These are: (1) The Bible clearly teaches us that Jesus calls children to himself, (2) Children open many homes for the gospel, and (3) The societal, religious, media, and family influences of today demand a Christian response.[20]

These three will be evident throughout the continuation of this writing. The challenge will be to lay a foundation of Scripture, then build philosophical walls which will stand the storms of time and societal pressure. Ideally, architecture of these arguments will compel the reader to reach and disciple children. George Barna notes, "We can strive to give our youngsters all the advantages the world has to offer, and motivate them to make the most of available opportunities and resources; but unless their spiritual life is prioritized and

---

19 Lebar, *Children in the Bible School*, 19–30 (See Appendix A).
20 Ibid.

nurtured, they will miss out on much of the meaning, purpose and joy in life."[21]

This work will propose the kind of holistic approach Barna has defined. The spiritual life of children must be prioritized and cultivated. It will be important for the reader to proceed with the understanding that spiritual life and growth is the ultimate aim of any outreach effort.

21 Barna, *Transforming Children*, 29.

CHAPTER 2
A BIBLICAL MANDATE

"God's blueprint for the dissemination of mankind always included children. Young ones were neither an addendum nor the result of the curse on Adam and Eve. God's command to be fruitful and multiply (Genesis 1:28) came before the fall."[1] In exploring the biblical mandate for evangelism of children, we must first recognize that God has always included children in His plan.

Baptist theologian William Hendricks writes of this saying, "An interpretation of biblical references to children would reveal the following conclusions. The childhood of important biblical figures is noted. Instruction of children by precept and example is commanded. There is a great compassion for the young displayed in biblical literature."[2] My objective in this chapter is to demonstrate God's desire that children be saved through the narrative and commands of Scripture.

It is the intent of God that all people young and old be saved. First Timothy 2:4 states that God "wants all people to be saved and to come to a knowledge of the truth." There is no

---

1   Robert J. Choun and Lawson, Michael, *The Christian Educators Handbook on Children's Ministry* (Grand Rapids: Baker Book Company, 1998), 16.

2   William L. Hendricks, *A Theology for Children* (Nashville: Broadman Press, 1980), 247.

age restriction on this or other salvation references in Scripture. One can assume that the gift of salvation is all-inclusive. God, who inspired John to write, "For God so loved the world that he gave his one and only Son, that whoever believes in him shall not perish but have eternal life,"[3] would scarcely leave the children out of the equation.

The age of accountability, which has been briefly discussed already, does not come into play in this discussion. Together, we will see that children and all other sinners are loved by God and will be forgiven by Him. We will show that God directs parents and other leaders to train the child from the time he is young.

This study of children in Scripture is not intended to be all-inclusive. It will focus on God's love and care for children, the responsibility of the parents and the church in regard to children, and the mandate to reach and disciple boys and girls. The stories of Old Testament children and parental directives to train children will be explored. Following this, Jesus' teaching concerning children and His encounters with children in the New Testament will be discussed.

Children in the Old Testament

Children were included in the corporate religious life of the Hebrew nation. Although they were not regarded as full-fledged members of the religious community, they were included in all readings, festivals, and community gatherings. Roy Honeycutt writes,

Within the legal sections of the Old Testament, there is a total absence of provisions about admitting children to full religious status. This is important, for the religious system carefully spelled out details about many other matters. The

---

3   John 3:16. See Matthew 18:14.

absence of rules in this area implies that, except for circumcision, children were accepted without going through any ritual or meeting any other requirements.[4]

But children were more than passive onlookers. God designed feasts and celebrations that included children actively. God intended history for the Hebrew culture to be a hands-on, participatory aspect of life. The children were to join in as, through feasts and celebrations, the community relived the past that helped shape its faith and identity.[5] Passover is probably the greatest example of this reliving of the past. In it, the children actively celebrate with family as they reenact events of their deliverance. Other festivals, including Tabernacles, Day of Atonement, and Rosh Hashanah, also provide times of remembrance and training of the children. The traditional practices woven into these festivals include storytelling, hands-on learning, prayers, repetition, Scripture reading, and total family involvement. It is known now that these kinds of methods are important when instilling faith in children. "The repeated cycle of week and year shaped the faith of the Mosaic community, affirming again and again the identity of the chosen people, and affirming again and again the identity of God as Creator and Redeemer."[6]

The Hebrew adult of the Old Testament assumes that children will grow up as active members of the community.[7] This is why children are present during the reading of the law in Joshua 8:35. This reads, "There was not a word of all that Moses had

---

4   Roy Honeycutt, "Children and Conversion," in *Children and Conversion*, ed. Clifford Ingle (Nashville: Broadman Press, 1970), 20.

5   Lawrence O. Richards, *Children's Ministry* (Grand Rapids: Zondervan Publishing, 1983), 21.

6   Ibid., 21.

7   Ibid., 20.

commanded that Joshua did not read to the whole assembly of Israel, including the women and children, and the foreigners who lived among them." One commentary says of this event, "The 'little ones' were to hear 'all that Moses commanded.' They might comprehend little. They would feel much. Through the imagination, their souls would be filled with abiding, restraining, and uplifting awe."[8] Children are included in the Hebrew community of faith. So much so, that they are even present during the judgment of Achan in Joshua 7.

As much as children lived as members of the Israelite faith community, God established the home as the primary component in nurturing their faith. This is established in specific detail in the verses following the *Shema Yisrael* in Deuteronomy 6:4. These verses (5–9), are commonly referred to as *V'ahavta*.[9] These verses read,

> Love the Lord your God with all your heart and with all your soul and with all your strength. These commandments that I give you today are to be upon your hearts. Impress them on your children. Talk about them when you sit at home and when you walk along the road, when you lie down and when you get up. Tie them as symbols on your hands and bind them on your foreheads. Write them on the doorframes of your houses and on your gates.

---

8   *The Biblical Illustrator* Copyright © 2002, 2003, 2006 Ages Software, Inc. and Biblesoft, Inc.

9   *Bible Knowledge Commentary/Old Testament* Copyright © 1983, 2000 Cook Communications Ministries; *Bible Knowledge Commentary/New Testament* Copyright © 1983, 2000 Cook Communications Ministries. All rights reserved. Deuteronomy 6:6–9 "God's people were responsible to meditate on these commandments, to keep them in their hearts. This enabled them to understand the Law and to apply it correctly. Then the parents were in a position to impress them on their children's hearts also. The moral and biblical education of the children was accomplished best not in a formal teaching period each day but when the parents, out of concern for their own lives as well as their children's, made God and His Word the natural topic of a conversation which might occur anywhere and anytime during the day."

There is in these verses a plan for intentional training of the children in which the parents become the primary religious educators. David Boyd shares, "Perhaps no biblical passage more clearly exemplifies God's mandate for intentional, systematic exposure of children to the Word of God and spiritual values."[10] The unique form of this instructional guide is clear in that it includes God's Word as authority, parent as teacher, and all of life as the classroom. Lawrence Richards reminds the reader, "Instruction is to infuse all of life, as parents share those truths of Scripture that are needed by a child to interpret his or her experiences."[11]

The pattern set forth in these passages includes responsibility, intentionality, creativity, and expectation.[12] *Responsibility* is demanded, as this training is not presented to parents as optional. Using words like "impress" and "talk," the writer assumes that parents will just do it. There is no formal request, informal suggestion, or question asked. Parents are simply exhorted to teach their children.

This is *intentional* in that training is be conversational and to take place in every life setting and situation. Children are to learn of God while walking along the road, lying in bed, or sitting around the table.

It is *creative* in that parents are exhorted to write these words on doorframes and gates. They are to tie them to their foreheads and on their hands. If modern parents would take this

---

10 David John Boyd, "The Church's Role in Building the Spiritual Foundation of Children" (Master's thesis, Assemblies of God Theological Seminary, 2006), 13.

11 Richards, *Children's Ministry*, 25. Richards amplifies this thought, saying, "Instruction is to be woven through the day, given as conversation about God's words as family members sit together at home, walk along the road, lie down at night, or rise in the morning. The underlying assumption seems to be that as life lived together, godly parents will explain their actions by pointing out the words of God that are guiding their responses."

12 Boyd, "The Church's Role," 13–15.

to heart, they would write Scripture on the refrigerator door and the dashboard of the family car. They would hang it on the bunk bed and in the family room. They would talk about it while waiting for the school bus and driving to soccer practice. The dinner table would become a place of devotion.

The *expectation* is that through these means, children would grow up to love the Lord their God with all heart, mind, soul, and strength.

Richards expounds on this idea: "If we were to adopt a similar pattern today we would seek to develop a ministry to children that: takes place in the context of a loving, holy community, features participation by children in the life of the community, and calls for instruction by and within the family unit."[13] Several authors refer to the placement of Scripture on the doorposts and gates as being "household memorials." Children and their parents were constantly reminded of God and His love for and commitment to His people.

One cannot discuss the place of children in Old Testament religion without visiting the memorial stones of Joshua chapter 4. The children of Israel had just crossed the Jordan at flood time. Before the priests left the middle of the river and the waters returned, Joshua sent twelve men, one from each tribe, to collect stones from where the priests had stood in the riverbed with the Ark of the Lord. These he set as a sign for the people. Then Joshua declares, "In the future, when your children ask you, 'What do these stones mean?' tell them that the flow of the Jordan was cut off before the ark of the covenant of the Lord. When it crossed the Jordan, the waters of the Jordan were cut off. These stones are to be a memorial to the people of Israel

---

13 Richards, *Children's Ministry*, 24.

forever."[14] The Hebrew word used here for memorial is *zakur*, meaning "to reflect on," "commemorate," "bring forth praise," or "be a remembrance."[15]

Of these stones, Keil and Delitzsch write, "It is not likely that they remained there for centuries; but they were intended rather as a memorial for the existing generation and their children, than for a later age, which would be perpetually reminded of the miraculous help of God."[16] Nonetheless, the stones were there when children and their parents crossed the river, went fishing, or just traveled by the spot. The act of setting the stones was also commemorated in the writing and the oral "tradition"[17] of the people, so in that sense, they have stood for countless generations.

Of this and other memorials in the life of Israel, Richards writes, "Memorials were another pervasive feature of the educational process woven by God into the fabric of ideal Israel. Throughout Palestine were multiplied reminders of Israel's heritage in the Lord: reminders each new generation could see and touch and feel."[18] Each of these memorials became an opportunity for curiosity to grow in children. They would inquire of their parents, asking, "What do these mean?" Mom and dad could then remind the children of what God did on that very spot. They could praise and thank God with their children and talk of God's goodness, faithfulness, and love for His people. The Lord had provided parents with a built-in devotional guide in the memorials of Israel.

---

14 Joshua 4:6–7.

15 Leslie C. Allen, "2349 (*zakur*)," in *New International Dictionary of Old Testament Theology and Exegesis,* ed. Willem A. VanGemeren 1. (Grand Rapids: Zondervan, 1997), 1100-1.

16 Keil and Delitzsch, *Commentary on the Old Testament: New Updated Edition,* Electronic Database. Copyright © 1996 by Hendrickson Publishers, Inc. All rights reserved.

17 Ibid.

18 Richards, *Children's Ministry,* 22.

There are many references throughout the Old Testament to children and the training of children. None is quite as poignant as the admonition of Psalm 78:1–8. This portion of Scripture establishes the importance of the oral tradition for the spiritual survival of the next generation. It reveals the generational importance present in the heart of God and His people Israel. Perhaps the psalmist had Judges 2:10 in mind when he penned these verses. It reads, "After that whole generation had been gathered to their fathers, another generation grew up, who knew neither the Lord nor what he had done for Israel."[19]

Psalm 78:1–8 reads,

> My people, hear my teaching; listen to the words of my mouth. I will open my mouth with a parable; I will utter hidden things, things from of old—what we have heard and known, things our ancestors have told us. We will not hide them from their descendants; we will tell the next generation the praiseworthy deeds of the Lord, his power, and the wonders he has done. He decreed statutes for Jacob and established the law in Israel, which he commanded our ancestors to teach their children, so the next generation would know them, even the children yet to be born, and they in turn would tell their children. Then they would put their trust in God and would not forget his deeds but would keep his commands. They would not be like their ancestors—a stubborn and rebellious generation, whose hearts were not loyal to God, whose spirits were not faithful to him.

There is a sense of urgency in these verses and in the narrative that follows concerning the insurance of the God-life being passed on to one's posterity. It is logical to surmise that if

---

19 Judges 2:10.

Hebrew fathers explained these things to their children, those children, when grown up, would not hide them from their own offspring.

There is a sense in this and other directives to parents throughout Scripture that God's desire is that spiritual heritage be passed down openly, honestly, and freely from generation to generation. This speaks of more than a Sabbath school or religious program. Fausset writes of this concept, indicating that training is to be accomplished, "Not merely by a formal teaching, but by speaking from the heart to their children's heart (Exodus 13:14; Deuteronomy 4:9, 23; 6:6–7)."[20] It is this heartfelt, emotionally charged spiritual passing of the baton that will affect change in a family, which in turn will change the nation.

Woven through the examples given is a thread of direction for the lives of children in the religious community. God has from the beginning loved and cared enough for children to provide them with spiritual mentors in the guise of parents. Tim Kimmel elaborates on this, "A family is, without doubt, the most effective and efficient vehicle to produce the kind of people who can move confidently into the adult world and have a redemptive impact on their culture—that's what we are supposed to be doing."[21]

That God has planned for heavenly relationship with all people regardless of age or moral understanding is continuous proof of His great loving-kindness. No one can doubt after viewing the place and presence of children in the Old Testament community and narrative that God loves kids. No

---

20 *Jamieson, Fausset, and Brown Commentary,* Electronic Database. Copyright © 1997, 2003, 2005, 2006 by Biblesoft, Inc. All rights reserved.

21 Tim Kimmel. *Grace Based Parenting: Set Your Family Free* (Nashville: Thomas Nelson, 2004), Kindle Locations 325-328. Kindle.

scholar of worth can dismiss God's plan for perpetuating His message and His people through the spiritual development of the child.

Children of the Old Testament

It is important now to briefly explore the living out of God's plan through the stories of individual Old Testament children. How did God work in their lives? What importance did spiritual mentors have in the prospect of these individuals perpetuating religiosity as they grew in age and in leadership? What childhood lessons caught by these children propelled them to spiritual significance?

Let's begin with the story of the boy Samuel. Scripture indicates that Samuel was dedicated to the Lord sometime after he was weaned. Honeycutt writes, "While there is no basis for assuming that this was the normal pattern, this is nonetheless a clear example of a child hardly beyond infancy who was taken to the shrine and dedicated to the Lord."[22] His parents dedicated him to the Lord, and Samuel grew up in the temple under the training of Eli. It will never be known how Eli treated Samuel different than his own sons. Perhaps he did his best to make up for the failings of raising his own children. Whatever happened, Samuel is found serving in the temple, ready to do whatever is asked of him.

Honeycutt writes of this story, "The Samuel narrative reveals two significant points. First, an individual could be dedicated to the Lord from infancy, and thus included in the broader circle of religious structures. Second, such an individual could have a new or special kind of experience—'Samuel did not yet know the Lord.'"[23]

---

22 Honeycutt, "Children and Conversion," 20.

23 Ibid.

One should consider the first point. It is significant in Scripture that children can be brought to the Lord and into His service at an early age. Although one doesn't find an overwhelming number of cases like Samuel's, it is important to note that nothing in this narrative points to his case being unusual. Neither Eli nor Samuel's parents though it strange to leave their boy in the temple service.

Honeycutt's second point concerning a new kind of experience once again reveals the special place God has in His heart for children. The boy is simply going about life, doing his best, when God enters the equation. Samuel is simply performing his regular duties and clearly has no expectation of revelation. His encounter with God is representative of the common association between temple and revelation. "Till that time Samuel had been employing himself in some good exercise or other, reading and prayer, or perhaps cleaning or making ready the holy place; and then went softly to his bed. Then we may expect God's gracious visits, when we are constant and diligent in our duty."[24]

And yet, God speaks to Samuel. It is clear that Samuel was going about his duties, learning about God and the temple, and did not expect a visitation from God. He was simply being faithful in the little things of life and God saw fit to give him much. One sees from this story that God will work in the lives of any who seek and faithfully serve Him, regardless of age. The Lord welcomes children and will work in and through their lives even in a time when His working is rarely witnessed.

Charles Spurgeon writes of the Samuel narrative, "Believe in the conversion of children, as children; believe that the Lord can

---

24 *Matthew Henry's Commentary on the Whole Bible*, PC Study Bible Formatted Electronic Database Copyright © 2006 by Biblesoft, Inc. All rights reserved.

call them by His grace, can renew their hearts, can give them a part and a lot among His people long before they reach the prime of life."[25] I have witnessed a genuine move of God in the lives of children as young as four and five years old. Young children often make a first-time commitment to Christ and, if allowed, will find and enjoy a place of simple service in the church.

Lawrence Richards pens, "The parents are to instruct, to model, and to discipline. The young are urged to accept, to heed, to remember, and to keep the parents' words."[26] But what is to become of the child who has no godly parents to instruct him in this manner?

To answer these questions consider 2 Kings, chapters 21–23, and the story of Josiah. One finds in the narrative that his father, Amon, "forsook the LORD, the God of his ancestors, and did not walk in obedience to him."[27] Amon dies and Josiah takes over at age eight. He reigns for thirty-one years, and Scripture says of him, "He did what was right in the eyes of the LORD and followed completely the ways of his father David, not turning aside to the right or to the left."[28]

Although Josiah's father was evil, little is known about his mother. Keil and Delitzsch suppose that, "As a child he had probably received a pious training from his mother; and when he had ascended the throne, after the early death of his god-less father, he was under the guidance of pious men who were faithfully devoted to the law of the Lord, and who turned his heart to the God of their fathers."[29]

---

25 C. H. Spurgeon, *Come Ye Children* (Pasadena: Pilgrim Publications, 1975), 81.

26 Richards. *Children's Ministry: formerly A Theology of Children's Ministry*, 27.

27 2 Kings 21:22.

28 2 Kings 22:2.

29 Keil and Delitzsch, *Commentary*.

It is probable that, like Joash of 2 Kings 12, Josiah did have godly counsel. It would hardly seem likely that a child of eight could have ruled against those advisors which surrounded him. What is notable in both his and Joash's stories is that a child in such a place could, and did, reign with godliness. Much of what these child-kings did affected the entire nation for God.

The challenge taken from this narrative is to guide children towards God and to see what He can do through their young lives. Space does not permit detail to be given of other Old Testament children. From Joash to the Hebrew children of Daniel 1:17, one finds God recognizing the worth of young people and blessing their lives.

Children in the New Testament

Coble writes concerning children in the Gospels, "The Greek word which is translated 'son' is used in the four Gospels over 220 times. Two related words which are usually translated 'child (children)' are used more than 50 times. Yet there are only five statements from Jesus' lips which make reference to children in a contemporary sense of the term."[30] Consider now a brief look at each of those five statements. The first two are what he refers to as minor references. This book will consider these first, then move on to the major teachings of Jesus concerning children.

In Luke 11:13 and Matthew 7:11 we find Jesus' teaching on prayer. He states in Luke, "If you then, though you are evil, know how to give good gifts to your children, how much more will your Father in heaven give the Holy Spirit to those who ask him!"[31] In Matthew "Holy Spirit" is exchanged with "good

---

30 William Coble, "New Testament Passages About Children," in *Children and Conversion*, ed. Clifford Ingle (Nashville: Broadman Press, 1970), 38.

31 Luke 11:13.

gifts."[32] Jesus, almost in passing here, comments on a fact of everyday life. Jesus capitalized on the fact that parents care for, love, and make provision for their children. This parental drive became a background for teaching the readiness and ability of the heavenly Father to love, care for, and provide for His children.[33]

This teaching is not so much aimed at evangelizing children as it is a comparison of earthly and heavenly parenting. In both cases one sees that the Father cares for and provides for His children. Scripture shows that wanting His children to be saved is in keeping with the heavenly Father's character.[34] Salvation is, after all, the highest form of provision.

The second minor text is that of Matthew 10:21–37. This teaching concerns the divisive possibility of the gospel in the family unit. Children may make choices for or against God which will be in conflict with parental choices. Coble writes, "Individual loyalty to Christ may cause a rupture of major earthly loyalties."[35]

There is no real case to be made for child evangelism from this passage other than to mention that a child may indeed choose Christ independent of his parent. This choice could subsequently cause conflict. Note here that neither one of these passages is promoting a parent-child relationship that is in conflict with the traditional Jewish family/religious unit. The first instance is observational and the second only a remote possibility.

There are three major teachings from Jesus concerning children. This study will first look at Jesus' blessing of the children

---

32 Matthew 7:11.

33 William Coble, *New Testament Passages*, 39.

34 Matthew 18:14.

35 William Coble, *New Testament Passages*, 39..

(Mark 10:13–16; Matthew 19:13–15; Luke 18:15–17). The paper will then view Jesus' teaching on greatness in the kingdom (Matthew 18:1–5; Mark 9:33–37; Luke 9:46–48). The document will end this section with a look at the teaching on the value of a child (Mark 9:42; Luke 17:1–2; Matthew 18:6–14).

In the first case, Jesus' blessing of the children is the classic motivational verse used by children's pastors and leaders to emote a response from seemingly non-caring congregants. Many have quoted, "Let the little children come to me and forbid them not . . ." with little regard to context or the entirety of the story.

People brought children to Jesus to be blessed. Coble says this was a "Jewish blessing that included the laying on of hands in a recognized ceremonial form."[36] He also goes on to say that the disciples' response was not surprising. "Outside of the home, the ancient world held a very low estimate of children. Usually the child was not even to be seen among adults, certainly not to be heard. An important Jewish leader was not expected to waste his time with children."[37]

Jesus' response was unexpected among his followers. After all, they were only attempting to protect the Master's schedule. But Jesus had scheduled an impromptu teaching. This episode in Jesus' ministry reflects the constant theme throughout the Gospels, especially in Matthew, that Jesus cares for the lowly, oppressed, and destitute of this world. Bruner writes, "The purpose of bringing children is Jesus' touch and prayer. This is still the purpose of the church's bringing the children to Jesus. This story is very useful. It teaches us that Christ does not receive

---

36 Ibid., 40.

37 Ibid., 41.

only those who voluntarily come to Him of holy desire and moved by faith, but also those who may not yet be old enough to realize how much they need his grace."[38]

Some have argued that the intent of this verse is not aimed at small children. Look at the Greek word used for little children in this passage. "Paidion (paidi/on—a diminutive of pais) signifies 'a little or young child'; it is used of an infant just born, John 16:21; of a male child recently born, e. g., Matt 2:8; Heb 11:23; of a more advanced child, Mark 9:24; of a son, John 4:49; of a girl, Mark 5:39, 40, 41; in the plural, of 'children,' e. g., Matt 14:21."[39] There is little doubt here that this story is about small children. Jesus would welcome the smallest child as He would any person. All are significant to Him. David Boyd writes of this, "To the disciples, children were an interruption. But to Jesus, children exemplified His receptivity to all people."[40]

This story is a reminder of God's everlasting love for every people group, every culture, every gender, every age level, and even the social misfits. Jesus' love for children is reflective, then, of His love for all.

Note the next story concerning true greatness in the kingdom:

> At that time the disciples came to Jesus and asked, "Who, then, is the greatest in the kingdom of heaven?" He called a little child to him, and placed the child among them. And he said: "Truly I tell you, unless you change and become like little children, you will never enter the kingdom of heaven. Therefore, whoever takes the lowly position of this child is

38 Frank Dale Bruner, *Matthew: A Commentary, Volume 2, The Church Book* (Dallas: Word Publishing, 1990), 694.

39 *Exegetical Dictionary of the New Testament* © 1990 by William B. Eerdmans Publishing Company. All rights reserved.

40 David John Boyd, "The Church's Role in Building the Spiritual Foundation of Children" (Master's thesis, Assemblies of God Theological Seminary, 2006), 13.

the greatest in the kingdom of heaven. And whoever welcomes one such child in my name welcomes me."[41]

Coble reminds the reader, "The age-old problem of man, the desire for recognition of rank, has always been a source of special problem in the Orient. The frequency of its appearance in the Gospels points to the seriousness of the problem, not only among the early apostles, but also throughout the early history of the church."[42] Jesus challenges this concept by using a child as an object lesson for His followers and for all.

One must be converted spiritually, but also attitudinally. One must learn to become a servant, live humbly, and be happy to give others first place. One must become dependent upon Jesus and others in this life of service. Children live in total dependence on parents and other caregivers. There is a consciousness of this dependence throughout childhood. One must establish that God consciousness which, like a child, causes total reliance upon the Lord.

Jesus makes a point as well that when we welcome a child in His name, we have welcomed Him. "In Christ's Kingdom one does not show supreme loyalty by saying to him, 'Your wish is my command.' That loyalty to Christ is shown when one meets one of the helpless and needy little children and acts out the motto, 'Your need is my Lord's command to me.'"[43]

Although this passage gives direction as to how the church should treat all children, it does not direct us specifically to evangelize them. Once again believers are left to contemplate an extended purpose in Christ's teaching. Would you allow any

---

41 Matthew 18:1–5.

42 William Coble, "New Testament Passages," 44.

43 Ibid.

child to go hungry, physically or spiritually? To do so would be to do this to Jesus. This is consistent with Christ's teaching in Matthew 25, "The King will reply, 'Truly I tell you, whatever you did for one of the least of these brothers and sisters of mine, you did for me.'"[44] Children certainly fall into the category of "least of these."

Hayes states, "To Him, the recovery of one lost child was top priority, and those who offended children were marked for judgment."[45] Reaching children with God's good news is practicing right actions towards His little ones.

Finally, look at Jesus' teaching on the value of the child. Mark 9:42 reads, "If anyone causes one of these little ones—those who believe in me—to stumble, it would be better for them if a large millstone were hung around their neck and they were thrown into the sea." We see in this statement great value placed on the child believer. Thomas Paterson writes of this verse, "Jesus has thrown his defense around childhood, and innocence, and trusted love, and who makes base assaults on these does so at eternal peril."[46]

There is some question among theologians as to whether this refers to actual children or new believers. Matthew's read on this teaching ends with specific reference to little ones. There is no mistake here. Matthew is referring to children. One already understands from this study that Matthew is concerned about the salvation and discipleship of all people.

Hayes reinforces this, saying, "We are reminded that every reference to children in the Gospels adds to our understanding of the gospel message. It is for all mankind, rich or poor, great

---

44 Matthew 25:40.

45 Edward L. Hayes, "Evangelism of Children," *Bibliotheca sacra* 132, no. 527 (July–September. 1975): 250.

46 Thomas Paterson, *Jesus and the Children: Winning Children for Christ,* ed. D.P. Thomson (New York: George Doran Company, 1925), 70.

or small, adult or child. 'Even so,' said Jesus, 'it is not the will of your Father which is in heaven, that one of these little ones should perish' (Matt. 18:14)."[47]

Children of the New Testament

The previous section briefly explored the teachings of Jesus in regard to children. Let us now briefly explore the children of Jesus' time. It is best to begin with Christ Himself. Little is known of the childhood of Christ other than the circumstances of His birth, His circumcision on the eighth day, and His trip to Jerusalem at age twelve. Jesus accompanied His parents to the feast as was the custom. Unbeknownst to His parents, as they began the journey home, Jesus was left behind. Once this was discovered, they began to search. After three days the child was found. Scripture says,

> After three days they found him in the temple courts, sitting among the teachers, listening to them and asking them questions. Everyone who heard him was amazed at his understanding and his answers. When his parents saw him, they were astonished. His mother said to him, "Son, why have you treated us like this? Your father and I have been anxiously searching for you." "Why were you searching for me?" he asked. "Didn't you know I had to be in my Father's house?"[48]

It seems evident from this interaction that at age twelve Jesus had a sense of His purpose on earth. *The Pulpit Commentary* suggests, "It was then, perhaps, as we have already reverently surmised, in the gradual development and growth of the Redeemer

---

47 Hayes, "Evangelism of Children," 253.
48 Luke 2:46–49.

that consciousness who he really was first dawned upon 'the Child Jesus.'"[49] One may never know the truth of this statement, but it is known that boy Jesus, after spending this time in the temple, returned home and obediently lived out His childhood and teen years. It would be eighteen years before Scripture once again picks up the narrative of Jesus' life. One can only speculate as to the kinds of life experiences He had during these years of silence. Scripture says during this time, "Jesus grew in wisdom and stature, and in favor with God and man."[50]

Jesus then launches into His public ministry. The Gospel writers mention a mere handful of encounters with children. This book has already cited stories of His standing a child in their midst and His blessing the children.

Although the account of five thousand being fed is recorded in each of the Gospels, it is John who indicates the involvement of a child. Andrew brings the boy and his lunch to Jesus' attention, saying, "Here is a boy with five small barley loaves and two small fish, but how far will they go among so many?"[51] No direct interaction is indicated in this passage. Nevertheless, the boy was brought forward with his lunch. One commentary says, "There is a lad here, the Greek word being *paidarion*—a little lad, probably one that used to follow this company."[52]

The boy was little and the lunch was real. He gave Jesus all he had. Several commentaries suggest that he may have been carrying this food for the disciples or selling the loaves and fish. "[There is a lad here] *Paidarion*, a little boy, or servant, probably

---

49 *The Pulpit Commentary*, Electronic Database. Copyright © 2001, 2003, 2005, 2006 by Biblesoft, Inc. All rights reserved.

50 Luke 2:52.

51 John 6:9.

52 *Matthew Henry's Commentary on the Whole Bible*, PC Study Bible Formatted Electronic Database Copyright © 2006 by Biblesoft, Inc. All rights reserved.

one who carried the apostles' provisions, or who came on purpose to sell his bread and fish."[53] That the child is mentioned is important. That his lunch was used is significant in that Jesus used the gift/lunch of a little boy to provide for the needs of over five thousand people. This story indicates that God can and will use children and their gifts to bless this world.

The possessed child of the Canaanite woman found in Matthew 15 and Mark 7 provides us with an example of Christ's compassion. He has a love for all people, children included, that reaches beyond borders and racial prejudice. The woman's little girl was healed by the word of Jesus. Adam Clarke's commentary gives us some insight on how complete the healing was. It reads, "The Æthiopic has a remarkable reading here, which gives a very different, and, I think, a better sense. And she found her daughter clothed, sitting upon the couch, and the demon gone out."[54]

The case of the demon-possessed boy found in Matthew 17 and Mark 9 demonstrates the power of Christ over evil and His concern for the helpless. When asked how long his son had been afflicted, the man answers, "from childhood,"[55] This young man had been possessed from the time he was a boy. He then turns to a description of the perils to which his child was continually exposed as a result of this evil possession.

It is important to note here that this and other descriptions of the demon possessed among children in the New Testament speak of the attack upon childhood found there and throughout history.

---

53 *Adam Clarke's Commentary*, Electronic Database. Copyright © 1996, 2003, 2005, 2006 by Biblesoft, Inc. All rights reserved.

54 Ibid., Mark 7:30.

55 Mark 9:21.

One last event which cannot be overlooked is the temple encounter of Matthew 21:14–16. Jesus had been healing people in the temple area when children began praising Him openly. "Jesus loved children, and they loved and followed him, taking up the cry which they had heard the day before from the multitude, and in simple faith applying it again to Christ. While grown men are silent or blaspheming, little children boldly sing his praises."[56] This writer has discovered that children love to bask in the presence of God. When children are exposed to Christ's love and power, they naturally wish to express their praise to Him.

Concluding Thoughts on the Biblical Mandate

The biblical mandate for reaching and discipling children includes a threefold approach. Children are included, invited, and instructed.

They are included throughout the Old and New Testaments in the community of faith. Lawrence Richards writes, "In the New Testament church, the Mosaic ideal of loving community began to be realized. Through the biblical description of those relationships and of the home, we can see a picture of the context in which Christian ministry to children first took place."[57] Children are present as the church meets in tents and later in homes. They are there when the law is read to the entire nation (Joshua 8:35), and when prayer is held (Acts 12:13).

Children are invited to take part in the plan of God. This is evidenced in God speaking to Samuel in the night (1 Samuel 3:1–15), using Naaman's servant girl in his healing (2 Kings 5:2), and Christ's teaching and example in Matthew 19:13–15.

---

56 *The Pulpit Commentary*, Electronic Database. Copyright © 2001, 2003, 2005, 2006 by Biblesoft, Inc. All rights reserved.

57 Richards, *Children's Ministry,* 45.

It is also apparent in the lack of age restrictions included within and around major salvation verses. Charles Spurgeon writes, "The Lord Jesus looks with pleasure upon those who feed His lambs, and nurse His babies; for it is not His will that any of these little ones should perish."[58]

Finally, this biblical mandate requires that children be instructed. This is clear in the *Shema Yisrael* and *V'ahavta*. Parental involvement in the faith training process is reinforced throughout the Old Testament. Proverbs 22:6, "Start children off on the way they should go, and even when they are old they will not turn from it," is a passage which reminds parents of their responsibility and ours to train the children. Psalm 78:1–8 gives clear direction for instructing children. It also develops a generational plan that can stretch from then until now. This plan includes parents telling and teaching their children about the Lord and the good things He has done. The reason given is found in verse 7. It reads, "Then they would put their trust in God and would not forget his deeds but would keep his commands."

The writer of Proverbs further emphasizes this theme when declaring that God's Word will help you live right. Almost quoting the *V'ahavta*, he states, "When you walk, they will guide you; when you sleep, they will watch over you; when you awake, they will speak to you."[59]

The New Testament church continued this pattern of religious instruction in the home and community. Children are present when Paul preaches in Acts 20:9 and prays on the beach in Acts 21:5. This threefold mandate holds true throughout Scripture. Children were, are, and should be included, invited, and instructed in the community of faith.

---

58 Spurgeon, "Come Ye Children," 59.

59 Proverbs 6:22.

CHAPTER 3
PERSPECTIVES ON EVANGELISM OF CHILDREN

The historical literature available concerning evangelizing and discipling children is as varied as the theological backgrounds of those producing the same. It is important to note that this author is writing from an Assemblies of God/Pentecostal perspective. This work regards other viewpoints, but the primary focus will turn the reader towards an A/G theological foundation concerning children and salvation. The Assemblies of God believes that "children are loved by God, and until they come to an age of understanding (some call it 'the age of accountability'), they have a place in the kingdom of God."[1]

It is commonly understood that only God can determine when a child has reached that point of understanding. Dr. Richard Dresselhaus writes, "Children, if properly taught, may at an early age enter into a personal relationship with Jesus Christ that will be very meaningful, both in childhood and in later life. The church must never under-emphasize the power of the Holy Spirit to produce saving faith in the heart of a child."[2]

---

1 Infant Baptism, Age of Accountability, Dedication of Children. http://www.ag.org/top/Beliefs/gendoct_11_accountability.cfm (accessed September 23, 2008).

2 Richard L. Dresselhaus, *Teaching for Decision* (Springfield: Gospel Publishing House, 1973), 60.

With this said, this study of the available literature regarding salvation and children will be broken down into historical/chronological segments. It will begin with pre-1900 writings and will be followed by a review of post-1900 works. The reader will find that the earlier writings follow either a tradition of salvation by baptism or that of salvation by familial association. As one progresses beyond the Reformation, writings take on a new theological approach adopted by the authors. This insists on the individual child being a sinner and coming to a point of conscious decision for or against Christ. Although the earlier theology is practiced to this day among Roman Catholics and others, when the divergence occurs, this writer will follow the salvation thread first noted by the Anabaptists and broadened into the evangelical tapestry one views in many of today's Protestant churches.

Pre-1900 Writings

The early writings of church fathers produce little for us to examine in regard to children and salvation. One cannot presume that the fathers did not care for children, but rather that in the context of their culture and understanding, children were accepted by God and trained in the Christian home by godly parents. Donald Joy further examines this. He writes, "In the early centuries of the church, no provision was made for the education of children, either in basic literacy or in Christian faith."[3] The virtual silence of the church fathers concerning children and salvation should not be interpreted too harshly. As in the Jewish culture from which the church emerged, family and home were primary in the religious upbringing of children. Lawrence Richards says of this, "While the early church carefully

---

3   Donald Joy, "Why Teach Children?" from *Childhood Education in the Church*, ed. Roy Zuck and Robert Clark (Chicago: Moody Press, 1975), 15.

designed rigorous catechetical systems for adult converts, it did nothing similar for its children. There were no agencies analogous to our Sunday schools."[4]

Though this is true, the early Christians did not neglect their children. On the contrary, they included them. Early Christians included children when they gathered. Children were included as attendees, not as formal members of the church.[5]

Justin Martyr wrote condemning the practices of exposing children, using them for sodomy, and selling them into slavery.[6] He also makes a case for the inclination that children have towards sin. This childhood sin is to be washed away through baptism.

> Since at our birth we were born without our own knowledge or choice, by our parents coming together, and were brought up in bad habits and wicked training; in order that we may not remain the children of necessity and of ignorance, but may become the children of choice and knowledge, and may obtain in the water the remission of sins formerly committed, there is pronounced over him who chooses to be born again, and has repented of his sins, the name of God the Father and Lord of the universe; he who leads to the laver the person that is to be washed calling him by this name alone.[7]

Tertullian admonishes the church, saying, "And so, according to the circumstances and disposition, and even age, of each

---

4   Lawrence O. Richards, *Children's Ministry* (Grand Rapids: Zondervan Publishing, 1983), 37.

5   Hugh Wamble, "Historic Practices Regarding Children," from *Children and Conversion*, ed. Clifford Ingle (Nashville: Broadman Press. 1970), 71.

6   Justin Martyr, *The Guilt of Exposing Children. Ante-Nicene Fathers, Volume 1,* PC Study Bible formatted electronic database by Biblesoft, Inc. Copyright © 2003, 2006.

7   Ibid.

individual, the delay of baptism is preferable; principally, however, in the case of little children."[8] Notice here that there is no push for infant baptism. It seems that the practice of infant baptism, and thus the accepting of the infant as "being saved," came later. One writer suggests, "That tradition was simply a convenient device for perpetuating Christendom."[9]

Augustine wrote volumes on doctrinal and philosophical arguments, leaving little doubt where he stood concerning these issues. When it comes to children, his literary voice is like an echo in an immense cathedral. Augustine does not talk so much of the salvation of children as he does the importance of baptism for both infants and adults. "For from the infant newly born to the old man bent with age, as there is none shut out from baptism, so there is none who in baptism does not die to sin. But infants die only to original sin; those who are older die also to all the sins which their evil lives have added to the sin which they brought with them."[10] Augustine does write concerning what he termed as the "non-innocence"[11]

---

8 Tertullian, *Of the Persons to Whom, and the Time When, Baptism is to Be Administered. Ante-Nicene Fathers, Volume 3,* PC Study Bible formatted electronic database by Biblesoft, Inc. Copyright © 2003, 2006. He further explains, "For why is it necessary—if (baptism itself) is not so necessary—that the sponsors likewise should be thrust into danger? Who both themselves, by reason of mortality, may fail to fulfil their promises, and may be disappointed by the development of an evil disposition, in those for whom they stood? The Lord does indeed say, 'Forbid them not to come unto me.' Let them 'come,' then, while they are growing up; let them 'come' while they are learning, while they are learning whither to come; let them become Christians when they have become able to know Christ. Why does the innocent period of life hasten to the 'remission of sins?' More caution will be exercised in worldly matters: so that one who is not trusted with earthly substance is trusted with divine! Let them know how to 'ask' for salvation, that you may seem (at least) to have given 'to him that asketh.'"

9 Bruce Shelley, *Church History in Plain Language* (Dallas: Word Publishing, 1982), 267.

10 Augustine, *Baptism and the Grace Which it Typifies are open to all, Both Infants and Adults from Nicene and Post-Nicene Fathers, Series 1, Volume 3,* PC Study Bible formatted electronic database. Copyright © 2003, 2006 by Biblesoft, Inc. All rights reserved.

11 Mary Ellen Stortz, "Where or when was your servant innocent? Augustine on Childhood," in *The Child in Christian Thought,* ed. Marcia Bunge (Grand Rapids: William Eerdmans Publishing Company, 2001), 82-83. "Between innocence and depravity Augustine

of childhood. The child is only pure in that he has not yet gained the capacity physically or mentally to sin. Once these barriers are overcome the child will do wrong. Augustine further argues that this inevitability of sin is accompanied by an increased accountability placed on the child as he/she grows into adolescence and adulthood. He writes, "With maturity and the acquisition of speech and reason, the non-innocence of an infant phased into the increasing accountability of childhood and adolescence. Greater accountability brought with it a greater sense of guilt."[12]

It can be argued from these writings that by Augustine's time, church leadership considered children capable of, and even accountable for, the commission of sin. The church did not begin a crusade for the wholesale evangelism of children in his time. Confirmation was adopted as an affirmation of the faith established in baptism. One author refers to confirmation as a "sacrament of initiation."[13] This became an appointed rite of passage in which the young person publicly acknowledges his guilt for sin and dependence on God for forgiveness. It also ties the child to the church through the symbolic, and in some cases actual, filling of the Holy Spirit. Confirmation can be likened to the Jewish Bar/Bat Mitzvah. The child, upon

---

posed a third possibility: non-innocence. Any innocence in childhood resided in physical weakness—that is, in being unable to harm anyone else *(In-nocens,* literally not harming)." and "Just as infants gain physical strength as they mature, so they assume greater accountability for their actions. A child learns to speak by associating sounds with objects, and speech introduces the ability to distinguish right from wrong."

12 Ibid., Augustine writes further on this subject, saying, "The meaning of accountability shifted throughout these three initial stages of the life cycle. While the infant's non-innocence might be judged pre-moral due to its lack of physical strength, the child's developing language skills conferred both an ability to communicate and increasing accountability for behavior. A child was held accountable if he or she violated a verbal rule."

13 Thomas Richstatter, *Sacraments of Initiation: Sacraments of Invitation* http://www.americancatholic.org/Newsletters/CU/ac0301.asp. (Accessed September 29, 2008).

reaching the age of reason, ceremonially chooses to enter the community of faith.

There appears to be no distinct beginning of this ritual. Early church fathers "considered that the rites of initiation (Baptism, the Holy Eucharist, and Confirmation) were instituted by Christ."[14] This sacrament was initially meant as a time when congregants sought the infilling of the Holy Spirit. Various terms and phrases were used which quite clearly refer to it. Thus, it is styled "imposition of hands" (*manuum impositio, cheirothesia*), "unction," "chrism," "sealing," etc.[15]

It is important to note for the purpose of this study that no mention is made by the early church fathers of children entering into this sacrament. It is my belief that as catechism grew from a ministry preparatory school to doctrinal training of the masses, children were eventually included.

Thomas Aquinas provided the church of his day with several arguments as to why children should not be received into religion. The foremost of these is that they are not of legal age. Aquinas writes, "No one should be tonsured unless he be of legal age and willing. But children, seemingly, are not of legal age; nor have they a will of their own, not having perfect use of reason. Therefore it seems that they ought not to be received in religion."[16] Thomas Aquinas points out that children are both not of legal age and that they have no will of their own.

For the purpose of contrast with Aquinas, this author challenges the reader to work one morning in a kindergarten Sunday

---

14 "Confirmation," *Catholic Encyclopedia Online.* http://ww.newadvent.org/cathen/04215b.htm (accessed September 29, 2008).

15 Ibid.

16 Thomas Aquinas, *Summa Theologiae,* PC Study Bible formatted electronic database. Copyright © 2003, 2006 Biblesoft, Inc.

school class. After serving thus, answer the question, "Do these children have a will of their own?"

Aquinas further argues that children cannot properly repent. He scribes, "Repentance does not become children. Therefore it seems that they should not enter religion."[17] One can observe even preschool-aged children in the home setting who, after following through with the temptation to hit another child with a toy, will look around with a face of guilt. That same child, after regular training in the home and church, will immediately recognize his wrong and apologize to the one wronged.

Aquinas, in his *Summa Theologica*, quotes Augustine, who wrote, "When little children are baptized, they die to that sin which they contracted in birth: so that to them also may be applied the words: 'We are buried together with Him by Baptism unto death'" (and he continues thus) "that as Christ is risen from the dead by the glory of the Father, so we also may walk in newness of life."[18] This shows the continued practice of infant baptism and its foundational underpinnings. It can be extrapolated from Thomas Aquinas's writings that he and the church of his time (1225-1274) believed that infants were to be accepted as being people of faith upon being baptized. Beyond that, children were not actively evangelized.

As this review moves ahead to the early 1500s, it finds Martin Luther addressing the subject of children and salvation. Luther taught that parents were to be apostles and bishops to their children. According to Luther, two of the primary responsibilities of parents were "to provide the sacrament of baptism for

---

17 Ibid.

18 Thomas Aquinas, *Summa Theologica*, "Whether Children Receive Grace and Virtue in Baptism," http://www.ccel.org/ccel/aquinas/summa.TP.iii.TP_Q68.TP_Q68_A9.html?highlight=children,augustine#highlight (accessed September 29, 2008).

infants and to form children in the true faith as they mature."[19] The attitude of the church towards children was still that of accepting them through baptism and purposing to allow parents to raise them in the faith.

To Luther, infant baptism signified a spiritual beginning that would be seen growing in the child as he matured. "Infant baptism becomes a measure for Luther of the graciousness of the gospel and the depth of the Christian community's trust in God to bring to fruition the good work God has initiated in the sacrament."[20] In Luther's *Table Talk*, he pens, "When Jesus Christ directed his apostles to go and instruct and baptize all nations, he meant not that children should be excluded: the apostles were to baptize all the Gentiles, young or old, great or small."[21]

This is representative of the continued emphasis that the church universal placed on the conversion/baptism of everybody, including infants and children. There was no requirement of prior faith experience or act of volition imposed upon the infant or child being baptized. Luther defends the practice of infant baptism while taking a shot at the Anabaptists.

The Anabaptists pretend that children, not as yet having reason, ought not to receive baptism. I answer: That reason

---

19 Jane Strohl, "The Child in Luther's Theology: For What Purpose do We Older Folks Exist, Other Than to Care for the Young?" in *The Child in Christian Thought*, ed. Marcia Bunge (Grand Rapids: William Eerdmans Publishing Company, 2001), 141.

20 Ibid., 142. This resource states further, "For an adult might deceive and come to Christ as a Judas and have himself baptized. But a child cannot deceive. He comes to Christ in baptism, as John came to him, and as children were brought to him, that his word and work might be effective in them, move them, and make them holy, because his word cannot be without fruit. Yet it has this effect alone in the child. Were it to fail here it would fail everywhere and be in vain, which is impossible. Thus infant baptism becomes a measure for Luther of the graciousness of the gospel and the depth of the Christian community's trust in God to bring to fruition the good work God has initiated in the sacrament. Having received the command to offer the gospel and baptism to everyone, the church must include children."

21 *The Table Talk of Martin Luther*, Translated by William Hazlitt. http://www.ccel.org/ccel/luther/tabletalk.i.html , CCCLI. (accessed September 18, 2008).

in no way contributes to faith. Nay, in that children are destitute of reason, they are all the more fit and proper recipients of baptism. For reason is the greatest enemy that faith has: it never comes to the aid of spiritual things, but—more frequently than not—struggles against the Divine Word, treating with contempt all that emanates from God. If God can communicate the Holy Ghost to grown persons, he can, *a fortiori*, communicate it to young children. Faith comes of the Word of God, when this is heard; little children hear that Word when they receive baptism, and therewith they receive also faith.[22]

Luther's logic was certainly a comfort to parents in his day. The logic is dependent on a special work of the Holy Spirit in the life of the child. It is also dependent upon an uninterrupted stream of Christian input in the life of a child. Luther's logic of reason disregards the impact of all other external forces and words spoken in the presence of the infant. What would keep the actions and words of an ungodly parent from having an effect that opposes that of Scripture in the faith life of the child?

Luther draws the Anabaptists into the discussion in a derogatory manner. This is not surprising, considering the persecution this group experienced from the Roman church as well as would-be reformers. It would appear from this author's research that the Anabaptists were the first religious movement to refuse the practice of infant baptism. "In 1525 one of the leaders of this new movement, Conrad Grebel, baptized a handful of followers in a home near Grossmünster."[23] It was around that same time that Grebel and his wife had a son born to them. Suddenly all of

---

22 Ibid.

23 William R. Estep, *The Anabaptist Story*. http://www.anabaptists.org/history/anastory.html (accessed September 29, 2008).

their theological theory faced the test of action. Would the baby be baptized? The Grebels refused, and other parents followed their example.[24] It is hard to say when the Anabaptists began to evangelize their children. It certainly had its beginning in the early days of their movement. The non-baptized unregenerate child was seen to have need of a Savior. After poring over several Anabaptist websites, it is apparent that today, as in the past, they place a high value on children and their education both in the church and community. "Since the child is alive to live forever, he has to be incredibly valuable. The redemptive life and death of the Son of God further enhances this intrinsic worth of the child."[25]

The literature reveals that within 200 years, children were encouraged to respond publicly during the Wesleyan revivals. "Wesley records in his journal several accounts of children who have had what he considers to be an authentic religious experience as early as the age of three."[26] The preachers of Wesley's day were somewhat divided on the place in eternity of the child who was not baptized. Some preached them right into hell, while others made allowance for the grace and goodness of God.

The important fact to note is that "Wesley presumes that a child can know God and thus be truly happy."[27] One finds that

---

24 Bruce Shelley, *Church History in Plain Language* (Dallas: Word Publishing, 1982), 268. The writer finds this account interesting. "In the early church, they said, men and women who had experienced personal spiritual regeneration were the only fit subjects for baptism. The apostolic churches knew nothing of the practice of baptizing infants." Grebel was quoted as saying, "That tradition was simply a convenient device for perpetuating Christendom, in a nominal but spiritually impotent society."

25 Mark Roth, *Seeing Your Child's Worth.* http://www.anabaptists.org/writings/kid-worth.html, 1995. (accessed September 29, 2008).

26 Richard P. Heitzenrater, "John Wesley and Children," in Bunge, Marcia J., *The Child in Christian Thought* (Grand Rapids: William Eerdmans Publishing Company, 2001), 295.

27 Ibid., 295. Many examples such as this one are recorded concerning the ministry of John Wesley. "Occasionally revivals broke out among children in the Methodist societies and at Kingswood school. Elizabeth Blackwell sent Wesley an account of one such revival

Wesley is open to the genuine conversion of a child and thus to the active evangelism of this people group. He was convinced that children would soon grow into sinners. They therefore were in need of grace.

At the same time that Wesley was observing the conversion of children, Jonathan Edwards (1703–1758) was preaching and seeing children respond. Probably the most well-known of these experiences was that of Phebe Bartlet. This four-year-old girl, whose eleven-year-old brother had been born again in an Edwards meeting, began a prayer vigil in her bedroom closet. She would wail in prayer, calling out to God for forgiveness. Phebe's parents called Edwards to their home, where he stood outside the closet listening to her pleas. Finally the child had a spiritual breakthrough, and in Edwards's own words, "Turning to her mother with a smile, she proclaimed, 'Mother, the kingdom of heaven is come to me.' In the hours and days afterward, Phebe seemed to have become a new creature."[28]

---

in Everton under John Berridge in 1759. Among those who experienced great spiritual struggle, and in some cases justification, were three young people, ages eight, ten, and twelve. The eight-year-old boy was said to have roared above his fellows and seemed in his agony to struggle with the strength of a grown man. John Walsh's account of this continuing revival a few weeks later includes notice of children, ages six and eight, who were crying aloud to God for mercy. He also notes that one eleven-year-old girl, who had been counted one of the wickedest in Harston, was exceedingly blessed with consolations of God, and a beggar girl of seven or eight felt the word of God as a two-edged sword and mourned to be covered with Christ's righteousness."

28 Catherine A. Brekus, "Children of Wrath, Children of Grace: Jonathan Edwards and the Puritan Culture of Child Rearing" in *The Child in Christian Thought* (Grand Rapids: William Eerdmans Publishing Company, 2001), 300. "In 1735, Jonathan Edwards (1703-1758), the pastor of the Congregational Church in Northampton, Massachusetts, was summoned to the house of a four-year-old girl named Phebe Bartlet. According to her parents, who earnestly sought his spiritual counsel, Phebe had undergone a remarkable religious change. Influenced by her eleven-year-old brother, who recently had been born again during a conversion experience, Phebe had begun to disappear into her closet to pray and weep for salvation. 'I pray, beg, pardon all my sins,' she was heard crying loudly to God." And later in the account it reads, "Turning to her mother with a smile, she proclaimed, 'Mother, the kingdom of heaven is come to me!' In the hours and days afterward, Phebe seemed to have become a new creature: she carefully recited her catechism, wept at the thought that her unconverted sisters might go to hell, and, like Augustine, repented for stealing some fruit—a handful of plums—from a neighbor's tree."

The personal involvement that Jonathan Edwards had in evangelizing children was a revelation to me. In his eyes, children represented the future of the church. They were born into sin and needed to come to Christ. "Edwards insisted that even the youngest children were corrupt unless they had been 'reborn' in Christ."[29] History records this famous revivalist, Jonathan Edwards, who not only accepted the possibility of a child conversion, but preached messages aimed directly at the children. One author writes, "In all of his sermons to children, Jonathan Edwards mixed clear, logical explanations of the Bible with emotional appeals to the heart."[30]

Edwards preached several sermons constructed just for children during the time of the Great Awakening. Although he preached messages that were understandable to children and painted a picture of a loving God, Edwards also did much to instill fear in the children. "To make children see their unworthiness, Edwards did not hesitate to use fear."[31]

To complete this look at pre-1900 writings concerning children and salvation, this book will review two final authors, Charles Spurgeon and Edward Hammond. These two seem to be representative of their times.

Charles H. Spurgeon (1834–1892) was an English Baptist preacher, author, and editor. Spurgeon was pastor of the Metropolitan Tabernacle in London from 1861 until his death. A collection of Spurgeon's writings and sermons regarding children can be found in a book entitled, *Come Ye Children*. In this collection Spurgeon writes, "Whether we teach young Christians truth or not the devil will be sure to teach them

---

29 Ibid., 304.

30 Ibid., 315.

31 Ibid., 316.

error."[32] To Spurgeon, the motivation for teaching children was also to bring them to Christ. He recognized that many churches in his day did not expect children to be saved, and thus saw no conversions among them. He observed that, "The conversion of children is not expected in many of our churches and congregations."[33]

Spurgeon also suggested an approach that set fear tactics aside in favor of Christian love and gentleness. He taught an almost cross-cultural approach to reaching children.

> Your mouth must find out the child's words so that the child may know what you mean; you must feel a child's feelings, so as to be his companion and friend; you must be a student of juvenile sin; you must be a sympathizer in juvenile trials; you must, so far as possible, enter into childhood's joys and grief. God will not raise a dead child by you if you are not willing to become all things to that child, if by any possibility you may win its soul.[34]

This shows that Spurgeon did not stop at inspiring and encouraging the parent and teacher to bring children to Jesus. He provided specific training in how to approach and win children. Spurgeon encouraged children's leaders, saying, "Before you can teach children, you must get the silver key of kindness to unlock their hearts and so secure their attention."[35] This certainly is an early example of a holistic approach to reaching and discipling children.

---

32 C. H. Spurgeon, *Come Ye Children* (Pasadena, TX: Pilgrim Publications, 1975), 9.

33 Ibid., 13.

34 Ibid., 157.

35 Ibid., 84.

Edward Payson Hammond was born in 1831 in Ellington, Connecticut. He worked with D. L. Moody in Chicago and traveled extensively, holding meetings in England, the Middle East, and parts of Europe. "In 1867 Hammond was instrumental in establishing the Children's Special Service Mission in London. He authored over a hundred books and tracts as well as composed many hymns."[36]

Hammond writes,

> All Christians of every name agree that "the wages of sin is death," and it must be admitted that, at as early an age as a child is capable of knowing right from wrong, it is capable of sinning. To defer the capacity for conversion to a more mature age than this, would be to leave to everlasting destruction all children past the age of sinning who die while they are too young to be converted.[37]

One can almost sense the urgent burden of this preacher across the waves of time. Hammond understands and articulates the need to reach children to a church that may not understand or agree with his premise. His is almost a twenty-first-century understanding that a child must be won when spiritual understanding awakens in his mind and heart. When expositing on Matthew 19:14, Hammond writes, "Are we not thus distinctly taught from God's own word that little children can intelligently believe in Christ?"[38]

Edward Payson Hammond provides both the church in his own age and the contemporary church with a benchmark work

---

36 Edward Payson Hammond. http://famousamericans.net/edwardpaysonhammond/ (accessed September 30, 2008).

37 Edward Payson Hammond, *The Conversion of Children* (New York: N. Tibbals and Sons, 1878), 5.

38 Ibid., 23.

in child evangelism. His book is inspirational balanced with practical application.

Post-1900 Writings

Frank Coleman's 1948 book, *The Romance of Winning Children,* is undoubtedly the single most important work on this subject written in the first half of the twentieth century. Most serious works concerning child evangelism following this book cite it in some manner. His teaching articulated the mainstream evangelical approach to child evangelism of his day. By Coleman's day there was little doubt among evangelicals that children should be reached and could consciously make a decision for Christ. He acknowledges this, saying, "Children can be saved. The Gospel message should not be denied them. We have a message which they can receive."[39]

In his introduction, Coleman writes, "No child should be left to grow up in our world of unbelief and flagrant sin without his having heard the Gospel with persuasive invitation to believe it and accept its salvation."[40] One can only imagine how Coleman would describe today's world. How much more persuasive would Coleman's appeal to today's lost child be in light of the current technological and physical availability of all manner of sin?

Two important arguments that Coleman makes for evangelizing children are the lifelong fruit redeemed in the born-again child and the absolute importance of ordinary Christians partaking in this venture. He writes, "Call the role of the saints of God who have led the forces of the church, who have pioneered

---

39 Frank G. Coleman, *The Romance of Winning Children* (Cleveland: Union Gospel Press, 1948), 22.

40 Ibid., 9.

in world missions, who have taught the people of God. The vast majority of them were saved in childhood days."[41] Reaching children is imperative to the future of today's church. Concerning the involvement of ordinary believers, he pens, "A great many Christians regard the [reaching] of children as a highly specialized ministry, demanding the services of a 'children's expert.'"[42] Boys and girls can be won to Christ by both the young enthusiastic creative genius and the old set-in-her-ways grandmother. The yielded saint with a love for God and the children can be that vessel which God uses.

Lois Lebar, professor of Christian Education at Wheaton College 1945–1975, was a prolific author and dynamic educator. Dozens of articles and three books are credited to her. Ms. Lebar's 1952 book, *Children in the Bible School*, was groundbreaking in both its philosophical and practical approach to childhood education in the church. In it Lebar writes,

> There is no larger soul value in the world than children. To impress boys and girls themselves with the value of giving their whole lives to Jesus, we sometimes ask them if they would keep an apple and not eat it until it has rotted, or an ice cream cone until it melts, or a new pair of shoes until they are too small or an automobile until it is rusted.[43]

Lebar provides persuasive reasons for the evangelization of children. One of these considers the readiness of children to accept the gospel message. In explaining this she notes, "Whereas many adults must be compelled to come to Christ,

---

41 Ibid., 10.

42 Ibid., 23.

43 Lois E. Lebar, *Children in the Bible School* (Old Tappan, NJ: Fleming H. Revell Company, 1952), 27.

the children are eager to come if only we adults get out of their way and let them come."[44] Her statement holds true to this day.

The research of George Barna supports this in that he reports that, "The probability of someone embracing Jesus as his or her Savior was 32% for those between the ages of 5 and 12; 4% for those in the 13 to 18 age range; and 6% for people 19 or older."[45]

Children still make up the largest, most reachable people group on planet earth. There is a readiness in children that has been worn off by the time they become adults.

Lebar's book stands out as an example of a number of Christian education works which include some talk of reaching children. Most manuals for Christian education include a smattering of information on evangelizing the young. Some specialty works for vacation Bible school or bus ministry also give a little information on how to reach the child. Some denominations, organizations, and individuals have published magazine articles, pamphlets, and single chapters in larger works rather than full books dealing with this vital area of evangelism.

An example of this is Lawrence Richards's book *Children's Ministry*. Published in 1983, this book covers a vast array of important concepts to consider when ministering to children. Concerning evangelism, Richards writes, "It would be wrong to deny the possibility of childhood conversion. But it would also be wrong to treat response by a child to an evangelistic appeal as an end in itself."[46] He then provides the reader with

---

44 Ibid., 20.

45 George Barna, *Transforming Children into Spiritual Champions* (Ventura: Regal Books, 2003), 34.

46 Richards, *Children's Ministry*, 375.

a relational approach to presenting salvation to and discipling children.

Randy Christensen finds a further example in the self-published work *Crucial Concepts in Children's Ministry*. In it Christensen writes, "Our role must be to fill kids' hearts and minds with the truth concerning our triune God, the all-powerful One! A relationship with Him will provide the spiritual satisfaction they desire. Nothing else will fill that void."[47]

It isn't until Sam Doherty's *How to Evangelize Children* is published in 2003 that we discover a new book dedicated wholly to child evangelism. Sam spent fifty years as a leader in Child Evangelism Fellowship in Ireland and Europe. He began writing training manuals and books in the 1990s as a way to pass on what he had learned during those years of ministry. Doherty is driven by a singular motivation summed up in the following paragraph:

> Children need to be evangelized. Boys and girls without Jesus Christ are spiritually dead, outside God's kingdom, and lost as far as their position is concerned. If they have reached the age of understanding and accountability (which is much earlier than most people think), and are not saved, they will, if they die, be lost forever.[48]

Doherty, like others mentioned earlier in this work, does not attempt to determine an exact moment when a child is accountable. He takes the position of our reaching all children so as to prevent any from going to hell. His desire to see children saved has provided volumes of material, including

---

47 Randy Christensen, *Crucial Concepts in Children's Ministry* (Tulsa: Insight Publications, 2003), 16.

48 Sam Doherty, *How to Evangelize Children* (Northern Ireland: CEF Specialized Book Ministry, 2003).

more than a dozen instructional books on evangelizing and discipling children.

Sam emphasizes a theme proposed by Frank Coleman in 1948. He says, "Experience also shows us that children can trust Christ. Many Christians, including a good number of pastors, missionaries, and well known Christians, date their conversion from childhood."[49] If the church were to acknowledge the numbers of influential believers won to Christ prior to the teen years, perhaps more finances and effort would be given to reaching children.

How to Evangelize Children provides the church with a very detailed manual for reaching children, including pointers for individual counseling as well as making appeals in large groups. Doherty writes concerning the giving of invitations for children to accept Christ. In answer to the question, "Should an invitation be given?" he responds,

> If you understand that the invitation is an essential part of the gospel message, then the answer is obvious. You will invite the children to come to Christ every time you preach and teach them the Gospel. The children who are listening to you should always know that Jesus Christ wants them to come to Him, to trust Him, how they can do so, and what the results will be, if they come.[50]

---

49 Ibid., 12.

50 Ibid., 59. Concerning invitations, Doherty also writes, "I never ask children to raise their hands, or look at me, or stand up, or come to the front if they want to be saved—or if they want to help them. This can easily result in a quick and emotional response which has not been thought through, or there might even be the possibility of following the leader, when children do what they see others doing. I personally feel that it is better to suggest to the children that if they want your help and counsel they come to you personally after the meeting is over. This allows them time to think about what they are doing and to come on their own initiative—rather than being influenced by others." (94).

Doherty also admonishes the church to adopt a big-picture attitude when approaching child evangelism. He writes, "World evangelism, or total evangelism, involves bringing the gospel to every tribe and nation, and also to every age-group—including children."[51] Missiologists have only recently come to recognize the importance of reaching the children. In the late 1980s Loren Triplet, then newly appointed leader of Assemblies of God World Missions, stated, "If I had it to do all over again in Latin America, I would begin with reaching the children."[52]

Dan Brewster, in a paper presented at Fuller Theological Seminary in 1996, coined the phrase *4/14 Window*, when referring to children ages four to fourteen as a people group that needed to be reached. Brewster wrote,

Cutting edge mission groups today are making some of the most significant advances in the history of Christianity by looking closely at the "10/40 Window." There is another "window within the window" however, which may be just as significant, and may enable many frontier missions' efforts to be even more effective. That window is what I call the "4/14 Window."[53]

Edward Hayes submits, "Jesus Himself said, 'Except ye be converted, and become as little children, ye shall not enter into the kingdom of heaven' (Matt. 18:3). To Him, the recovery of one lost child was top priority, and those who offended children were marked for judgment."[54] God's priority has always been children. His "top priority" has never changed.

---

51 Ibid., 17.

52 The author personally heard this in Reverend Triplet's address to the General Council in Oklahoma City.

53 Dan Brewster, "The 4-14 Window, Children and Missions Strategy" (Lecture, Fuller Theological Seminary, 1996).

54 Edward L Hayes, "Evangelism of Children," *Bibliotheca sacra* 132, no. 527 (July–Sept.

Those considering the possibility of evangelizing children must consider God's desire in this venture. Lining your will up with God's will in this matter will send you to the ends of the earth proclaiming Jesus to children. David Boyd writes, "Scripture distinctly teaches God's commands of intentionally passing on spiritual faith to the next generation. Children clearly receive insight, direction, and power from God when given proper instruction and opportunities to do so."[55]

One recent work encouraging the church to consider reaching children is George Barna's *Transforming Children into Spiritual Champions*. In it, Barna draws from statistical analysis of his surveys on children in the church when approaching the subject of evangelizing children. Concerning childhood, Barna challenges the reader, "If you want to shape a person's life—whether you are most concerned about his or her moral, spiritual, physical, intellectual, emotional or economic development—it is during these crucial eight years that lifelong habits, values, beliefs and attitudes are formed."[56] Children are the most vulnerable and reachable members of our society. Barna's writings echo those of Charles Spurgeon, Frank Coleman, and Lois Lebar.

Barna also makes an argument for impacting the world through children's ministry. He says, "The research reinforces one simple but profound truth over and over again: If you want to have a lasting influence upon the world, you must invest in people's lives; and if you want to maximize that investment, then you must invest in those people while they are young."[57]

1975): 250–264.

55 David John Boyd, "The Church's Role in Building the Spiritual Foundation of Children" (Master's thesis, Assemblies of God Theological Seminary, 2006), 22.

56 Barna, *Transforming Children*, 18.

57 Ibid., 42.

But Barna further exhorts the church leader to recognize the intrinsic value of children. They are not to be considered loss leaders in the realm of Christendom.

Barna's book provides the twenty-first-century pastor with solid statistical, biblical, and philosophical arguments for reaching and discipling children. He emphasizes both the church and the family participating together to train little ones. Barna also provides examples of congregations which have taken up and begun to run with the baton of children's ministries. In summing up the importance of the church partnering with parents in raising spiritual champions, Barna submits, "Invariably, the churches where the children's ministry prospers are those led by pastors who are unapologetic advocates for that ministry focus."[58]

There is one other aspect of children's evangelism that Barna touches on which others rarely mention: children evangelizing children. He is proposing a profound effectiveness intrinsic to peer evangelism. Barna writes, "We have discovered that peer evangelism among young children—one kid leading another kid to the foot of the cross for a life-changing encounter with Jesus—is one of the most prolific and effective means of evangelism in the nation."[59]

I can personally testify to what Barna is suggesting. Sandi,[60] a young girl who attends a local children's church, has brought at least three friends to church over the past couple of years. Each of these girls has given her life to Christ as a result of Sandi's efforts.

---

58 Ibid., 104.

59 Ibid. 49.

60 This name has been changed.

Jon, age ten, prayed for five friends from school over a period of several months. He then presented each with the gospel message one week and personally led three of the five boys to Christ. Sandi and Jon are just two examples of the many children I have known who have carried out the Great Commission with the fervor and seriousness of a seasoned missionary.

We cannot complete a literature review on the evangelism of children without making some observations concerning the Sunday school movement. Robert Raikes launched the modern Sunday school movement in Gloucester, England. In 1780 Raikes began the first school.[61] Raikes had failed to make a difference in the lives of adult prisoners that he ministered to, so he began to reach out to the children. He believed that he could change a nation through the children. Children of that day worked six days a week. That left Sunday as the only day that Robert could impact the youth. Edgerly writes, "On the Sabbath the uneducated children caroused, drank, and created havoc. Raikes hired a teacher, paid the children a penny if they came with clean hands, and encouraged them to be taught the basics of reading, writing, and morals using the Bible as the text."[62]

The concept was at first discouraged by church leaders, but eventually men like John Wesley got behind it. By 1784, over 240,000 students were enrolled in Sunday school in England.[63] Sunday school was so successful under Wesley's leadership that

---

61 Wayne Widder, "Reviewing Historical Foundations," *Christian Education: Foundations for the Future*, ed. by Robert Clark, Lin Johnson, and Allyn K. Sloat (Chicago: Moody Press. 1991), 53.

62 George Edgerly, Efraim Espinoza, and Steve Mills, *Focus on Administration: A Handbook for Leaders.* (Springfield: Gospel Publishing House, 1993), 5.

63 Wayne Widder, Wayne. "Reviewing Historical Foundations," 53.

George Whitfield commented on it. Read this account of Whitfield's opinion of Sunday school.

Wesley's contemporary, George Whitfield, drew larger crowds and had more converts. However, later in life, Whitfield wrote, "My friend Wesley was the wiser. He joined his converts into classes and thus conserved the fruit of his ministry. But alas, I did not do so. Today my followers are as a rope of sand."[64]

Sunday school spread worldwide and is the most common vehicle used in evangelism and discipleship ministry to children. Although the form of Sunday school is constantly changing, small group, age-level appropriate Bible study is flourishing in the church world. Barna points out that "41% of the people who attend the church on a typical weekend are under the age of 18."[65] These young people are attending classes geared to their age level. It is in these that many will discover pre-evangelism feelings towards God, the church, and the Bible. Here is where many will make a first-time commitment to Christ, which will then be supported by the church and family.

Concluding Thoughts on Perspectives

The perspectives reviewed reveal that church leaders from Jesus' time until now have cared for the eternal destiny of boys and girls. Although the approach has been, and is still, varied, it is generally accepted that a child, whether born with sin or a leaning toward it, will sin. Only Jesus can cleanse them from this sin. It has been shown that the family tree of child evangelism branches off when the Anabaptists refused to baptize their infants. From that time on, those who set aside the practice have

---

64 George Edgerly, Efraim Espinoza, and Steve Mills, *Focus on Administration: A Handbook for Leaders.* (Springfield: Gospel Publishing House, 1993), 6.

65 Barna, *Transforming Children*, 40.

dedicated resources to presenting the gospel to children. Children of all ages have been encouraged to commit their lives to Christ.

David Boyd, National BGMC Coordinator for the Assemblies of God, shares that there are "numerous twentieth-century writings which document that spiritual fervor within children did not simply occur during Bible times. Children today have the opportunity to powerfully experience 'divine moments' with God that will change their lives forever."[66]

Children can and will be saved when the church opens its doors and its arms to the little ones. Once they have made that first-time commitment to Christ, the church must support them in an ongoing discipleship process. Lawrence Richards pens, "The real challenge in ministry with boys and girls is to provide that context in which the first step can be taken . . . and then a whole lifetime of growth be supported."[67]

---

66 Boyd, "The Church's Role," 16.
67 Richards, *Children's Ministry*, 374.

CHAPTER 4

A PRACTICAL RESPONSE

Any practical response to the biblical mandate and philosophical foundation for evangelizing children must give thought to how the modern church will include, invite, and instruct children. Lawrence Richards challenges the church to adapt its approach while considering the impact of the surrounding culture. He says,

> It seems clear that the living faith to which the Christian community is called demands the ability to apply biblical truth in a constantly changing world, where many varied associations of biblical principles with changing situations is vital. It also seems clear that children are able to generate spiritual insights that they arrive at intuitively, which can be expressed in true faith responses.[1]

If the church is to be an agent of change in the lives of children, it must provide atmosphere and opportunity for children to intuitively generate positive spiritual insights. This can begin to happen in the traditional Sunday school or children's church.

---

1 Lawrence O. Richards, *Children's Ministry* (Grand Rapids: Zondervan Publishing, 1983), 120.

But it cannot be limited to the one to three hours a child spends in the church building each week. The church must work with parents, reaching into the life and the home of the child in order to have lasting impact. Paul wrote of this when he penned, "We loved you so much, we were delighted to share with you not only the gospel of God, but our lives as well."[2] This verse speaks of a love that drives the leader beyond the classroom walls and into the life of the learner. This must begin with prayer.

Any consideration given to the church's response to, and implementation of, the Great Commission as it regards children must take into consideration the cultural texts of childhood. Such a study must include a reflection on the psycho-cultural impact of broken families, childhood fears, and media input. It must then generate foundational principles for a holistic approach to reaching and discipling children. This work will now discuss how the church can include, invite, and instruct children.

Include

"Those who care about children will make a deep commitment and provide long-term relationships and endless love that make faith community God's unique context for His kind of ministry with boys and girls."[3] This is a challenge to the church to move beyond that initial verbal commitment to Christ as the end-all in children's ministries. Children need a lifelong relationship with loving adults who will continuously model Christian living for them. In Ivy Beckwith's *Postmodern Children's Ministry*, she writes,

---

2   1 Thessalonians 2:8.

3   Lawrence O. Richards, *Children's Ministry* (Grand Rapids: Zondervan Publishing, 1983), 375.

I believe the time has come for churches to reconsider the overt evangelization of children. The approaches typically used have little or no bearing on what's actually happening in a child's heart and mind. For the most part these tactics are manipulative, playing on the child's emotions and desire to be accepted and loved. A faith community should never be involved in manipulating the soul of a child.[4]

To better understand how to move from this type of spiritual manipulation to godly inclusion, one must begin to understand who children are and what they face in the American culture.

Beckwith defines this group of postmodern children who darken the doorsteps of our churches each week. She then theorizes how the church can reach this generation. Postmodern children are not inclined to believe that God and His truth undergird all that is. To them, truth is subjective. Reality is interpreted through life experience rather than scriptural foundations. A postmodern believes that there is no standard outside of ourselves, and our community helps us determine what is right and wrong.[5]

Ministers serve a group of people who are growing into, or already are, postmodern thinkers. The media, peer influencers, and educators with this postmodern message of tolerance are pummeling the children they meet week by week. Richard Dobbins warns, "Even the National Commission on Mental Health of Children has said that those who go into adult life without a clearly defined set of values are more likely to be overwhelmed emotionally. That's why it's so important that

---

4   Ivy Beckwith, *Postmodern Children's Ministry* (Grand Rapids: Zondervan, 2004), 65.
5   Ibid., 25.

children are taught the bedrock of values on which the Church has stood for 2,000 years."[6]

It is not adequate that the minister only understand who children are. One must also understand what they face on a daily basis. The Children's Defense Fund reports that on any given day in America,

Every 25 seconds a child is arrested.

Every 36 seconds a child is confirmed as abused or neglected.

Every minute a baby is born to a teen mother.

Every 9 minutes a child is arrested for a violent crime.

Every 18 minutes a baby dies before his first birthday.

Every 5 hours a child or teen commits suicide.

Every 6 hours a child is killed by abuse or neglect.[7]

Child abuse and neglect is at epidemic proportions in our culture today. Wayne and Diane Tesch, in their 2008 book, *From Despair to Heir: Reviving the Heart of a Child*, write, "Statistics show that one in four adult women and one in six adult men were abused as children."[8] This means that there are abused and neglected children in every Sunday school class and children's service. Those whom ministers and volunteers serve alongside of may have been abused as children. The tragedy of child abuse is its generational implications. Tesch writes, "Individuals who suffered abuse as children may forever deal with the emotional and physical scars it leaves. These scars can cripple their relation-

---

6   Richard Dobbins, *Troubling Questions For Troubling Times.* http://www.drdobbins.com/articles/article.php?article=9&topic=10 (accessed September 6, 2008).

7   Children's Defense Fund website. http://www.childrensdefense.org/site/PageServer?pagename=research_national_data_moments (accessed September 5, 2008). See Appendix D.

8   Wayne Tesch and Diane Tesch, *From Despair to Heir: Reviving the Heart of a Child.* (Santa Ana: Royal Family Kid's Camps, 2008), 28.

ships, self-esteem, and their future if they do not get help. One act of abuse can leave a scar in the mind and heart of a person for a lifetime."[9] The church that wishes to have an eternal impact on children must not ignore the abused and neglected children of their church and community. This writer proposes that the church recognize and respond to the needs of abused and neglected children.

Abuse is only one way that childhood is under attack in America today. In his book, *The Hurried Child*, noted psychologist and author David Elkind introduces the theme that children in this society are being hurried to grow up too fast. Media, peers, parents, and educational systems are rushing children into an unhealthy adulthood. Elkind writes, "Childhood has its own way of seeing, thinking, and feeling, and nothing is more foolish than to try to substitute ours for theirs."[10] In making the point that adults pressure children to grow up too fast, Elkind poses, "It is a unique characteristic of contemporary society that we burden our preschoolers with the expectations and anxieties normally visited upon high school seniors."[11] This rush to force children to grow up has multiplied in its groundswell since Elkind wrote this book.

One cannot overlook the effect of divorce on children's lives. Hara Estroff Marano writes in *Psychology Today*, "Divorce undermines kids' sense of trust and causes them great psychological distress as they grow. They have trouble forming relationships of their own, and are particularly unhappy as adults."[12] It is generally

---

9   Ibid., 29.

10   David Elkind, *The Hurried Child* (Reading, CA: Addison-Wesley Publishing Company, 1981), 4.

11   Ibid., 35.

12   Hara Estroff Marano, "Honey, Let's Get Divorced," *Psychology Today* http://www.psychologytoday.com/articles/pto-19990501-000038.html (accessed September 5, 2008).

understood in ministry circles that divorce is divergent to raising healthy children, both spiritually and emotionally. Richard Dobbins writes, "The people who really suffer in a divorce are the children."[13]

In light of this troubling information, what can the church do to include children? Richards suggests that it develop a relational climate in which children can grow closer to God. He says, "We can never overestimate the importance of the relational climate. This climate is perhaps the most powerful single influence in child development. Wrapped in the love of parents and valued by other adults in the close-knit faith community, each child was gently guided to and nurtured in faith."[14] The picture painted here is one of the child being gently guided. This kind of approach must consider a child's basic needs. The church should develop a practical approach to theology and childhood that in focusing on a religious conversion does not lose sight of the need to generate an effective holistic ministry before, during, and beyond the conversion experience.[15]

Children are whole beings. When their basic needs such as food, drink, security, and friendship are met, children will more readily respond to Christian teaching.

An inclusive plan to reaching children must be approached as a partnership with parents. Robert Choun writes, "A growing awareness of God takes time. The practice of truth is like piano practice; both take incalculable repetition to achieve proficiency. Children have qualities that require that kind of attention and repetition."[16] This kind of growing awareness can only take place

---

13 Richard Dobbins, "Divorce," http://www.drdobbins.com/articles/article.php?article=10&topic=10 (accessed September 5, 2008).

14 Richards, *Children's Ministry*, 47.

15 William L. Hendricks, *A Theology for Children* (Nashville: Broadman Press, 1980), 234.

16 Robert J. Choun and Lawson, Michael S., *The Christian Educators Handbook on Children's Ministry* (Grand Rapids: Baker Book Company, 1998), 35.

in the child's life as the church and the parent work synchronically, presenting a consistent message of redemption. Brian Dollar pens, "God's plan is for parents to be the primary spiritual leaders of their children; our role is to support them and equip them."[17]

Note again the story of Jesus. In Luke 2, He returned home, obediently living with Mary and Joseph. It is under their guidance that He grows in wisdom and stature and favor with God and with man. Perhaps today's church should revisit this approach. Beckwith reminds all, "Parents and churches who are truly interested in the positive soul care of the child will not be as concerned about this one-time experience as they will about ongoing immersion of the child in the things of God and Jesus."[18] This ongoing immersion by necessity must take place in the home, with the church becoming a center of reinforcement. Too often, children and parents are separated in the church setting, and this kind of reinforcement has no opportunity to take root. Beckwith goes on to caution the church leadership, saying,

> Many large churches talk about having good age-related, segregated children's programs because this attracts adults to their ministries. The large attendance numbers these churches crave are built on programs that have little to do with the soul care of the children, little to do with supporting families, and everything to do with giving the consumer what he wants.[19]

If one is to follow the biblical mandate to include the children, the church must seek to understand today's child and revisit

---

17 Brian Dollar, *I Blew It* (Springfield, MO: Influence Resources, 2012), 105.

18 Ivy Beckwith, *Postmodern Children's Ministry*, 62.

19 Ibid., 104.

basic methodology for the evangelism, care, and discipleship of boys and girls. It is imperative that the church seek out new ways to involve and train parents, become a resource and support station for families, and integrate proactive relational ministry to this important people group.

Invite

"As soon as children begin coming to church, we tell them they must have a personal relationship with Jesus Christ. We give altar calls in each Sunday school class, Royal Rangers meeting, and Missionettes meeting."[20] There is no doubt that Pastor Barnett's motives are pure. He is a soul winner who wants to see boys and girls come to Christ. One does not call into question the motivation or methodology so much as the implementation of these. The traditional invitation or altar call enacted by a well-meaning teacher may do little to ensure that children are actually coming to a saving knowledge of Jesus. Oftentimes pressure is applied for response. The church must engage in evangelistic efforts which include times of commitment, but caution must be exercised. Edward Hayes pens, "Avoid anxiety-producing appeals to both parents and children."[21]

Children's Pastor Randy Christensen has traveled extensively across the United States preaching in camps and crusades. He exhorts, "The church must learn to see children with God's eternal view instead of seeing them as immature pre-adults

---

20 Tommy Barnett, Earl Banning, Peter Hohmann, and Jay Hostetler, "Mobilizing a Millennial Generation," *Enrichment*, no. 2 (Spring 1999), 21.

21 Edward L. Hayes, "Evangelism of Children," *Bibliotheca sacra* 132, no. 527 (July–Sept. 1975): 258. Hayes also writes, "Often a child responds to a gospel appeal out of a deep desire to gain approval. It is part of the identity struggle within each of us to desire the approval of a parent or teacher. Winning the child according to this set of psychological principles, may be little more than instilling into the child the mysterious codes and mores of our society. Thus, willingly obedient, a child may gain his rightful place in the family or other adult institutions."

who must wait to make a difference as part of the kingdom. Children are now eternal souls. They are not distractions to be removed from the sanctuary, nor caterpillar saints, who must go through a metamorphosis in the church basement before they can become citizens of God's kingdom."[22]

Many have sought to win children through public invitations. Oftentimes, there is an overwhelming response among children to such a call. Some rightly credit this to the work of the Holy Spirit. But others have observed the use of fear, crowd psychology, or abundant excitement to draw in the net of children. In his 1987 book, *How to Lead a Child to Christ*, Daniel Smith instructs, "Fear or any other strong emotion wrongly used can cause us to run ahead of the Holy Spirit and precipitate a false profession. A certain amount of emotion is normal and healthy in response to the gospel, but we can overdo playing upon emotion to the detriment of the child."[23]

The church must discover ways to invite children to become members of God's kingdom that take into consideration their unique season of life. Boys and girls can, through genuine conversion, become full-fledged members of the faith community. One may now wonder whether to even give an invitation.

Sam Doherty addresses the possibility of pressuring children into a premature or nonexistent commitment and in practice gives no formal public invitation.[24] Instead, he recommends, "It is better to suggest to the children that if they want your help and counsel they come to you personally after the meeting is

---

22 Randy Christensen, *Crucial Concepts in Children's Ministry* (Tulsa: Insight Publications, 2003), 32.

23 Daniel H. Smith, *How to Lead a Child to Christ* (Chicago: Moody Press, 1987), 34.

24 Ibid., 94. "I never ask children to raise their hands, or look at me, or stand up, or come to the front if they want to be saved—or if they want me to help them. This can easily result in a quick and emotional response which has not been thought through, or there might even be the possibility of following the leader, when children do what they see others doing."

over. This allows them time to think about what they are doing and to come on their own initiative—rather than being influenced by others."[25]

Doherty is building a decision time with the child that is constructed on more than the emotion of the moment. He builds relationship with the children, presents the good news to them in a creative, participatory manner, and gives the opportunity to come to Jesus without pressure.

The decision or response time must be understood as a starting point. "It would be wrong to treat response by a child to an appeal as an end in itself. Instead we need to focus our attention on providing children with a place within a vital faith community in which they can come to know Jesus and be brought naturally to readiness to respond when God the Spirit does His work in their lives."[26]

Children must have an opportunity to come to Christ. But that opportunity should never be forced, play upon their emotions, or emphasize the need to please the leader or the peer group. Will the child understand the entirety of what is accomplished when accepting Christ as Savior and Lord? Probably not. The challenge is for any adult reader to fully comprehend the work of the cross and resurrection. Richards assists us in understanding what happens when a child responds to the invitation. He says, "We ought to consider the possibility of children giving a true faith response to God without a formal understanding of what is involved in our formulations of the gospel. A child's simple response to Jesus may be analogous to the faith response of so many through history who have not understood the cross, but

---

25 Ibid.

26 Richards, *Children's Ministry*, 375.

who have met God in the more simple Word He spoke to them, and who have believed."[27]

The biblical mandate to invite children stands. Jesus encourages us in the pages of Scripture and across the pages of time to "Let the little children come."[28] God's desire that all men be saved transcends age barriers. The church must invite children to come in a way that reveals its understanding of childhood and its trust in God.

Instruct

The biblical order to instruct or train a child is probably the clearest directive given concerning children. This emphasis occurs over and over again throughout the Old Testament. The culture of the New Testament enforces this with Scriptures like, "Fathers, do not exasperate your children; instead, bring them up in the training and instruction of the Lord."[29] George Barna challenges the church, saying, "We can strive to give our youngsters all the advantages the world has to offer, and motivate them to make the most of available opportunities and resources; but unless their spiritual life is prioritized and nurtured, they will miss out on much of the meaning, purpose and joy in life."[30]

In a society where children are given most everything they desire, what can the church do to instruct them in the ways of God? How can the church teach children in ways that will inspire them to come to Jesus?

---

27 Ibid., 375.

28 Matthew 19:14.

29 Ephesians 6:4.

30 George Barna, *Transforming Children into Spiritual Champions* (Ventura: Regal Books, 2003), 29.

Beckwith postulates that the training arm of the Christian church in America is broken. She writes,

> It's broken when church leaders and senior pastors see children's ministry primarily as a marketing tool. It's broken when we teach the Bible as if it were just another book of moral fables or stories of great heroes. Something's broken when we trivialize God to our children. It's broken when we exclude children from perhaps the most important of community activities: worship. It's broken because we've become dependent on an 18th century schooling model, forgetting that much of a child's spiritual formation is affective, active, and intuitive.[31]

We must seek to comprehend today's child, and then gear our teaching so that it is synchronized with his capacity to comprehend.[32] So the wise leader will study children and childhood within the cultural texts. He will then design a Christian education system within his sphere of influence that takes into consideration the real needs of children, the role of the parents, and the place of the faith community in the process.

Once a plan is developed, the church must provide the finances and personnel to see the plan implemented. Barna chastises the church, saying, "Less than 15% of the average church's ministry budget is allocated to the needs of children's ministry."[33]

---

31 Ivy Beckwith, *Postmodern Children's Ministry*, 13.

32 Richards, *Children's Ministry*, 91. Richards goes on to demonstrate a possible pattern for childhood education. This is established by considering Comenius' definition of the steps of nature: "1) Instruction must begin early and before the mind is corrupted. 2) The minds must be made ready for it. 3) It must proceed from the general to the particular, and 4) from easier to the more difficult. 5) Progress must not be rushed. 6) The minds must not be forced to do anything but that to which they aspire according to their age and motivation. 7) Everything must be applied immediately, and 9) Everything must be taught consistently according to one and the same method."

33 Barna, *Transforming Children*, 40.

More money must be allocated to the instruction of children and to the training of adults in biblical parenting.

Instructing children in the Lord is an all-important task that the church cannot afford to shy away from. If this present generation is to grow up believing and knowing why they believe, the church must continue to improve its approach. Instruction of the young must become a priority.

Concluding Thoughts on the Practical Response

"Perhaps the church has erred in focusing attention upon salvation words rather than on a meaningful relationship with Jesus Christ."[34] Let the church not be guilty of error when it comes to including, inviting, and instructing children. This important segment of the faith community must be nurtured if the church is to remain healthy. This generation is part of today's church, and is in training to lead the church of tomorrow. If they are to grow into leadership, they must understand the message of the gospel. Boyd reminds us, "What children cannot understand, cannot change their lives. Capable children's leaders utilize language, concepts, and phrases on the child's level of understanding. This does not mean leaders avoid difficult scriptural principles; rather they strive to utilize understandable concepts to convey deeper meanings."[35]

The challenge for child evangelism and retention in this century is for leaders to enter into this important aspect of Christian community with open hearts. They must develop vibrant ministries that include all in the community of faith. They

---

34 Richard L. Dresselhaus, *Teaching for Decision* (Springfield: Gospel Publishing House, 1973), 59.

35 David John Boyd, "The Church's Role in Building the Spiritual Foundation of Children" (Master's thesis, Assemblies of God Theological Seminary, 2006), 46.

must not shy away from invitation, but present the good news in ways that children will understand and embrace of their own volition. Finally, they must approach the instruction of children with a firm understanding of childhood in our culture and how to best inspire these little ones to continually come to Jesus.

Up to this point, this work has not investigated the incredible variety of methodologies that are being utilized in children's evangelism today. I pray that this has provided you with a foundation for the evangelism of children upon which vibrant ministries utilizing age-appropriate messages and methods can be built. I wish that you would do all you can to win many children for Christ. I hope that in doing so, you will develop discipleship programs that partner with parents as children grow in their newfound faith.

CHAPTER 5

ETHICAL CONSIDERATIONS WHEN GIVING ALTAR CALLS TO CHILDREN

Introduction

The idea for this chapter began to germinate in my mind in May of 2002. I was sitting in a recliner on the deck of the Disney Magic cruise ship in the harbor at Saint Thomas. I sat there, with the umbrella shading me from the tropical sun, reading Sam Doherty's book *How to Evangelize Children*. I came to the part that read, "I never ask children to raise their hands, or look at me, or stand up, or come to the front if they want to be saved. This can easily result in a quick and emotional response which has not been thought through, or there might even be the possibility of following the leader, when children do what they see others doing."[1]

I couldn't believe it. This guy was promoting a children's sermon that ended without the traditional evangelical altar call. At first I was taken aback by the thought, but the more I pondered it, the more Sam made sense.

I have served in children's ministry since the spring of 1975. In this time, I have participated both alongside of the children

---

1   Sam Doherty, *How to Evangelize Children* (Northern Ireland: CEF Specialized Book Ministry, 2003), 94.

and as the leader during countless altar services. I have seen children come to Christ and have experienced the sweet presence of the Holy Spirit filling children to overflowing. I have participated in many prayer services where children have been saved, healed, and delivered at altars.

It is not about these sweet times that I write today. For the purpose of deeper study and increased enlightenment in the area of altar calls and children, I begin by focusing on the negative side of altar calls and children.

Matthew 19:14 reads, "Jesus said, 'Let the little children come to me, and do not hinder them.'" He did not say, "Drag, coerce, push, force, threaten, or browbeat them to come to me." Over the years, altar calls for and with children have included many different styles, uses, and, sad to say, abuses. I have witnessed people holding children down until they received the baptism in the Holy Spirit. At one camp an adult was shaking a child by the shoulders and demanding that the child receive the baptism. I have even heard an agitated altar worker yelling at children to repeat phrases in order to be filled with the Spirit. It should be obvious to you that these practices are abusive and out of place.

In 1878, Edward P. Hammond wrote, "The devil knows how much easier it is to get children to come to Jesus than the old hardened sinner. Therefore it is that I believe he is the more keenly on the alert when any attempt is made in this direction."[2]

I do not doubt the sincerity of Hammond's words or the possibility of satanic disruption of the direction and intent of altar calls and altar services. Some of what I have seen could scarcely be conjured up by human design alone. Much of what I view as abuses of the altar call and the child participants may

---

2   Edward Payson Hammond, *The Conversion Of Children* (New York: N. Tibbals and Sons, 1878), 19.

not be credited to the enemy of our souls, but rather to the ignorance or innocence of the altar leader. Had that person been confronted with a few simple ethical imperatives prior to leading the service, his approach and the results may have done more to glorify God and bless the child.

It is my assertion that a positive ethical approach can be made to this important aspect of ministry to children. The altar call given without ethical consideration may do more harm to the children present than good. Some aspects of an ethical approach have already been touched on earlier in this book. This chapter expands on those themes.

I will begin this hike down the trail of ethical considerations by looking at an ethical response to the age of accountability. This will be followed by three segments addressing: (1) Faith or Fear; Setting aside scare tactics and letting God be God, (2) Pressure or Pleasure; Relaxing the altar time so that children can enjoy the presence of God, and (3) Let or Limit; Allowing children to come to Jesus rather than engaging in psycho-spiritual coercion.

I trust that by the end of this work, you will have a better understanding of ethical considerations in giving altar calls to children. It is my prayer that in better understanding these topics, you who read will endeavor to lead altar times with children in a godly, loving manner.

An Ethical Response to the Age of Accountability

Although the "age of accountability" is not so much an ethical question as a theological one, I felt that this work could not proceed without some thought given to this subject and our ethical response. Let me remind you of what has been covered earlier while adding to those observations.

The Bible does not use the term "age of accountability," nor does it imply that there is one mystical age frame during which children suddenly understand and are drawn to a decision for or against God. Edward Hayes writes, "An 'age of accountability' is not taught in the Scriptures. In fact, the basis for it is only a logical inference. If we accept the biblical teaching of original sin as related to an Adamic nature, we infer that the infant is born in sin, needs divine grace, and is ultimately accountable for that sin."[3] The inference in our movement always leans towards the person, young or old, being a sinner in need of God's grace. I am partial to William Hendricks's teaching as he states, "The term 'age of accountability' means a time or period of life when one is aware enough of God's presence to respond to Him."[4]

The question always arises, at what time can a child become aware enough to be saved? How old must he be before we teach him to love Scripture and the message it brings?

Irish children's leader Sam Doherty penned, "The Bible does not give an age, and neither should we. Children differ from each other. But the Lord Jesus did speak about little ones trusting him (Matthew 18:6). So the age when a child can trust Christ is generally much lower than what many Christians believe."[5] The age of a child may very well be a factor, but in my experience conscious accountability has more to do with maturity level than chronological age. Assemblies of God Pastor Richard Dresselhaus tells us in his 1973 book, *Teaching for Decision*,

---

3   Edward L. Hayes, "Evangelism of Children," *Bibliotheca sacra* 132, no. 527 (July–September 1975): 250–264.

4   William Hendricks "The Age of Accountability," in *Children and Conversion*, ed. Clifford Ingle (Nashville, Tennessee: Broadman Press, 1970), 84.

5   Doherty, *How to Evangelize*, 12.

Obviously, it is impossible to determine a uniform age when all children reach this point of awareness. The rate of growth and maturity varies radically, according to ability and background. Some children have a basic comprehension of the gospel at age four or five. Others may reach the age of ten before they seem ready to grasp the message of the gospel. At any rate, salvation is conditioned upon some ability to understand the basic plan of salvation. This is true for children as well as adults.[6]

My own children professed Christ as Savior for the first time at ages three through five. Granted, each one had a different understanding. I do not believe that my children understood justification or the substitutionary atonement. But each one understood God's love as demonstrated through parental love and reinforced by loving teachers and leaders in the church. The message, "Jesus loves me this I know," was pretty much all they needed for that first-time profession of faith.

William Hendricks shows us this when he writes, "Tests of children's alertness and ability are illustrating that children mature at different ages and according to their individual capacity. This fact does away with all attempts to establish a given and fixed chronological age as the time of accountability."[7]

So we've established that there is no designated age of accountability in Scripture and that sometime in childhood, people reach an age of awareness and are therefore accountable to God. Lawrence Richards declares, "We ought to consider the possibility of children giving a true faith response to God without formal understanding of what is involved in our formulations of

---

6   Richard L. Dresselhaus, *Teaching for Decision* (Springfield, MO: Gospel Publishing House, 1973), 57.

7   Hendricks, "The Age of Accountability," 90.

the gospel. A child's simple response to Jesus may be analogous to the faith response of so many through history who have not understood the cross, but who have met God in the more simple Word he spoke to them, and who have believed."[8]

We have also come to the juncture where ethics come into play. If we are uncertain as to when a child can understand and accept salvation, then we have an ethical responsibility to do what we can to see that child come to Christ at as early an age as possible. Let me put it another way: if a child reaches the age of accountability and does not accept Christ as Savior, that child may spend eternity without Christ. He may go to hell. Our ethical imperative, as it relates to the age of accountability, is to present the gospel to all children so they have the opportunity to make a decision for salvation.

This begins with the church involving itself in pre-evangelism training of the young children. From the time they are born, we can begin to surround them with the message of God's love. This happens as caring, loving workers serve the children week after week. All of this time, the church is reinforcing what is happening in the home. Lawrence Richards emphasizes this when he interjects, "We can never overestimate the importance of the relational climate. This climate is perhaps the most powerful single influence in child development. Wrapped in the love of parents and valued by other adults in the close-knit faith community, each child was gently guided to and nurtured in faith."[9]

Can we allow boys and girls the possibility of spending eternity in hell? The answer is, "certainly not!" But we must heed the challenge that Rick Chromey presents, "Children's

---

8   Lawrence O. Richards, *Children's Ministry* (Grand Rapids: Zondervan Publishing, 1983), 375.

9   Richards, *Children's Ministry,* 47.

ministries in the 21st century will reinvent themselves around relationships, images, and experiences that are 24/7/365, where faith is a personal, dynamic journey."[10] Our task is to facilitate this personal dynamic journey. This begs the question, "How?"

My first response is that we cannot force this issue. "Transformation is a work of the Holy Spirit alone. All we can do is to help facilitate that process. Much of the time that means we, as adults, need to get out of the way so that the Spirit of God can do that work."[11] So the Holy Spirit must work, but children's leaders must be used in His work. God chooses to use us in this grand salvation scheme. Scottie May and her team tell us, "God grants us the privilege of partnering with the Holy Spirit in helping children come and see Jesus. We can point children to Jesus by helping them enter the stories of Scripture and follow Jesus there, getting to know him, love, and believe in him."[12]

We become eternal tour guides, pointing children to Jesus as they walk this road of life. The leader in the Sunday school, small group, or children's church must take seriously the need for salvation of the children. I met a children's church leader once who admitted that in three years he had never given a salvation invitation in his church time. The kids had enjoyed teaching, puppets, and games, but had never been given the opportunity to respond to a loving Savior. Dresselhaus reminds this worker and others like him, "Only through a careful teaching of the Word of God, and as the Spirit is active, will these children recognize their need and feel drawn by the Spirit to salvation."[13]

---

10 Rick Chromey, "The times They Are A Chaingin'" in *Children's Ministry in the 21st Century* (Loveland, CO: Group Publishing, 2007), 12.

11 Scottie May, Beth Poterski, Catherine Stonehouse, and Linda Cannell, *Children Matter* (Grand Rapids: William Eerdmans Publishing, 2005), 24.

12 Ibid., 70.

13 Dresselhaus, *Teaching for Decision*, 56.

Our ethical response must not be to give altar calls for the sake of numbers. Nor can it be driven by the possible guilt of losing children to a Christ-less eternity. Instead, we must be driven by love for children and the leading of the Spirit to bless the kids and, with God's help, win them for Him before their hearts become old and cold. We must, with enthusiasm and godly wisdom, present the gospel in ways that boys and girls will understand. If we fail in this, we would be ethically negligent.

The church must do all it can so when that individual time of accountability comes, we can walk the child into God's presence. "The time of accountability is the moment of grace when one is brought to a decision for or against Christ by the Spirit. This moment requires the proclamation of the Word, the drawing of the Spirit, and the yielding of the individual to God. Until this moment is possible, one may leave children in the hands of God."[14]

We must proclaim the Word to children through godly settings, relationships, and programming. We teach with a sensitivity to the Spirit's leading and yield ourselves to God. Then when the child reaches an appropriate level of accountability, the salvation step taken can be both meaningful and eternal.

Faith or Fear; Setting aside scare tactics and letting God be God

Daniel Smith writes, "Perhaps one reason so many children go into a period of spiritual stagnation in their teens is that they were frightened into 'jumping on a fire escape' rather than being warmly attracted to the Person of Christ. Although the danger of a lost eternity is a part of the gospel, it is not the central issue."[15]

---

14 Hendricks, "The Age of Accountability," 97.
15 Daniel H. Smith, *How to Lead a Child to Christ* (Chicago: Moody Press, 1987), 21.

It was the first kids' camp I had ever attended. I was a counselor for twelve elementary-aged boys. We sat through the long Monday evening service. My boys were restless and tired. Some were sleeping.

Suddenly, the lighting changed and the leader began drawing a colorful chalk picture on a large drawing board. Dynamic music played in the background. The leader spoke as he drew. He told the story of a drawbridge operator who, in order to save an entire trainload of passengers, killed his only son in the gears of the drawbridge. This man then invited children to accept the sacrifice of Jesus. I witnessed children crying as they went to that altar rail. For the most part, the Holy Spirit did not convict them. They were scared by a story. They were full of sorrow for the boy who had been killed.

Smith informs us, "Both Scripture (1 John 4:18) as well as personal experience teach us that fear is a powerful and uncomfortable emotion."[16] Our task in leading children to the altar should not be one of frightening them. We are presenting a loving God who will accept them in their sinful state, forgive them, and cleanse and befriend them for eternity.

Since that first camp experience, I have experienced many similar altar services. These were services during which the leader played upon the emotions of children, causing them to fear for their eternal destination as well as their livelihood on earth. One night at a camp in the Midwest, a children's worker laughed and said to me, "That preacher sure scared the hell out of them, didn't he?" I did not find this funny. There is no solid ethical platform from which I can preach that would allow me to "scare the hell out of them."

---

16 Ibid., 20.

Edward Hayes reinforces this concept as he notes, "Avoid anxiety-producing appeals to both parents and children. In any effort to evangelize children, youth, or adults, the Scriptures give us the clues. We are to balance our zeal with confidence in a sovereign God."[17] It would seem to me that a preacher who preys upon the fears of children in order to reap a harvest has little confidence in a sovereign God.

I know of a man who performs great feats of magic in his services. Early in his ministry, he used intense colors, lights, and actions to preach his message of salvation. Much of this frightened the children and disturbed the adults. As he grew in the Lord and in his ministry, the man simplified his program, making it less scary and more understandable at the same time. He essentially did what H. B. London wrote about when he inscribed these words: "The Church can be the place where the child feels safe, cherished, and nurtured."[18] Casting fear into a crowd of children is not the kind of net that reaps an authentic spiritual catch. Jesus, our Good Shepherd and master fisher of men, would use bait and tackle that fit the waters in which he was fishing.

My friend Randy Christensen writes, "Children are searching for the reality of supernatural power in an everyday world. This is the theme of the most popular children's books, movies, and toys."[19] In our current spiritual climate, children are being subjected to all kinds of interpretations of the use and misuse of spiritual power. Every character from SpongeBob to Harry Potter is using magical interaction in some form to entertain.

---

17 Hayes, "Evangelism of Children," 258.

18 H. B. London and Neil Wiseman, "A Wake Up Call to Save Our Children," *Enrichment*, 4, no. 2 (Spring 1999), 16.

19 Christensen, Randy, *Crucial Concepts in Children's Ministry* (Tulsa, OK: Insight Publications, 2003), 16.

The church must be a place where genuine spiritual power is demonstrated in a non-abusive, Christlike manner.

Robert Choun puts it beautifully when he pens, "A growing awareness of God takes time. The practice of truth is like piano practice; both take incalculable repetition to achieve proficiency. Children have qualities that require that kind of attention and repetition."[20] Fear tactics to reap results at an altar are little more than an attempt to bypass a God-imposed natural order and rush children to a verbal commitment before their hearts are ready for salvation. It's like placing them in a piano recital without having allowed time for practice.

So let us reiterate the ethical consideration here. The leader of children must put aside personal ambition and rely on faith rather than fear in giving altar calls to children. He must set aside scare tactics and let God be God. The leader must, with a clean conscience, present the facts of the gospel in a consistent, understandable way to the children. Witnessing positive spiritual results in the lives of children may take minutes, days, or even years. In this respect, children's ministry is not a sprint, but rather a marathon.

Sam Doherty shows us this, saying, "As you evangelize children you should instruct the mind, praying that God will enlighten it; involve the emotions, praying that God will stir them; and challenge the will, praying that God will change its direction."[21] The key element in what Sam says is "God." Notice his total reliance upon God for results. In Sam's words, "God will enlighten, God will stir, and God will change its direction." The task then is to allow God to do His work and will in the

---

20 Robert J. Choun and Michael S. Lawson, *The Christian Educators Handbook on Children's Ministry* (Grand Rapids, MI: Baker Book Company, 1998.),17.

21 Doherty, *How to Evangelize,* 22.

life of the child as you faithfully present God's Word and plan to that child.

When altar time comes, put away your arsenal of scary and heartbreaking stories and replace them with a kind invitation to accept God's forgiveness and grace.

Pressure or Pleasure; Relaxing the altar time so that children can enjoy the presence of God

> Often a child responds to a gospel appeal out of a deep desire to gain approval. It is part of the identity struggle within each of us to desire the approval of a parent or teacher. Winning the child according to this set of psychological principles may be little more than instilling into the child the mysterious codes and mores of our society. Thus, willingly obedient, a child may gain his rightful place in the family or other adult institutions.[22]

Our treatment of altar calls and ethical considerations would not be complete without addressing the pressure that can accompany an appeal for salvation. Perceived pressure, whether valid or not, may drive a child to a response without the wooing of the Spirit. The child may have learned, through regular observance, that those who accept Christ find communal approval. Pressure to "get saved" is translated into acceptance in the church family, which is very appealing to children. Well-meaning, and perhaps spiritual, workers may inadvertently apply pressure promoting this kind of "approval conversion" experience among the children.

In the midst of this possible atmosphere of underlying community pressure, we must continue to encourage individual children in the faith. Daniel Smith reminds us, "There is no more biblical basis for doubting the genuine, intelligent, and *unforced*

---

22 Hayes, "Evangelism of Children," 257.

confession of faith from a child than there is from an adult."[23] Kids can be genuinely saved in spite of a presence of pressure.

Smith goes on to say, "No doubt many boys and girls are unwisely urged into a false profession. But spiritually minded adults who know the Word of God and love children can discern genuine confessions by careful communication with children."[24] We must begin to sort out the sheep in the pen, discovering just what kind of conversion experience they have enjoyed. Children should not be left without guidance as they progress from whatever level of faith they have achieved. Pastor Richard Dresselhaus writes, "Children, if properly taught, may at an early age enter into a personal relationship with Jesus Christ that will be very meaningful, both in childhood and in later life. The church must never under-emphasize the power of the Holy Spirit to produce saving faith in the heart of a child."[25]

Our ethical approach demands that we "properly teach" the children. Our approach must never be one of compelling commitments, pressuring young children, or demanding through our actions and words that the altar be filled. "Make appeals for young children to receive Christ that are prompted by pure motives and are given simply and in a nonpublic manner. The notable success of various child evangelism efforts cannot be denied. But the motive must never be numbers or outward response, nor should appeals be accompanied by offers of gifts, recognition, or special privileges."[26]

Our challenge is to relax the altar call so that children can respond to and enjoy the presence of God. It was Monday night

---

23 Daniel H. Smith, *How to Lead a Child to Christ,* 15.

24 Ibid., 15.

25 Dresselhaus, *Teaching for Decision,* 60.

26 Hayes, "Evangelism of Children," 259.

altar time at a camp in Texas. A boy named Mike approached me and declared, "I am not going to pray." Rather than force his involvement, I was checked by the Spirit and answered, "Well just sit back and watch then. If you have any questions, come see me." Mike almost seemed confused by my answer and worked his way through the other children back to his seat. This same scenario was repeated the following two nights, and finally on Thursday evening, Mike came up to me with tears in his eyes. He blurted out, "I want to pray. I know I need Jesus." Had I forced Mike's involvement, he may have rejected Christ altogether.

An invitation to come to Christ need not be forced or pressure-filled. Children can be encouraged to act upon what they have learned in a service without adults and other children applying undue pressure to respond.

Sam Doherty instructs us in the importance and style of the gospel invitation given to children. He exhorts, "The invitation is a call from Jesus Christ to come to him, in repentance and faith, to receive forgiveness and a new nature."[27] This is a loving invitation to come to Christ. It is a gentle, encouraging word instructing the unregenerate child to admit his sin and trust Jesus for forgiveness and new life. There are no clamps of guilt pressing down on the child. There must be no words or actions that make the child feel less than accepted if he does not respond.

As Doherty teaches children's workers using examples from the book of Acts, he explains, "Like the apostles, you should trust God the Holy Spirit to work in the hearts of the children—and not put pressure of any kind on them to respond to Christ's invitation."[28] So our task in approaching altar calls

---

27 Doherty, *How to Evangelize,* 55.

28 Ibid., 61.

in an ethically responsible manner is to relieve the pressure. Evaluate methodology used to gain a response and develop a process that allows children to come to Jesus without social or emotional screws being tightened.

This brings us to our final consideration.

Let or Limit; Allowing children to come to Jesus rather than engaging in psycho-spiritual coercion

The key question here is, "How are you, as a leader of children, going to follow the words of Jesus?" Is it possible to "let" the children come without engaging in forms of coercion? I believe it is. I come full circle back to the original quote that inspired my study of the approach to altar calls and children. "I never ask children to raise their hands, or look at me, or stand up, or come to the front if they want to be saved—or if they want me to help them. This can easily result in a quick and emotional response which has not been thought through, or there might even be the possibility of following the leader, when children do what they see others doing."[29] This generates the question, can an altar call be given without application of psychological, social, or spiritual coercion?

Sam proposes that rather than altar calls, the children's worker give invitations. He suggests that the leader invite the child to come and seek counsel after the meeting is over. "This allows them time to think about what they are doing and to come on their own initiative—rather than being influenced by others."[30]

I am not suggesting that the children's leader give up the tradition of the altar call. What I am suggesting is that we utilize this important juncture in any service to impart a loving invi-

29 Ibid., 94.
30 Ibid., 94.

tation to children. This invitation may or may not include the children coming forward in response. Whether this invitation includes an immediate public response or not is the leader's prerogative. It must carry with it authority without pushiness and spirituality without overzealousness.

The altar call or invitation must not water down the basic gospel message. Tony Kummer, Baptist children's pastor, blogs, "Being overzealous to give a child assurance of heaven can result in a false assurance. Repentance is a biblical component of conversion."[31] Sound teaching on basic salvation doctrine is demonstrated through the life of the teacher, then acted upon by the child. This suggests more of an ongoing process rather than a onetime, instant occurrence. Lawrence Richards expounds upon this, saying, "Ultimately, our assurance of a relationship with God does not come because we remember when we made a verbal commitment, but because we increasingly commit ourselves to live for Him, and discover a growing trust and love. It would be wrong to deny the possibility of childhood conversion."[32] He writes further, "The real challenge in ministry with boys and girls is to provide that context in which the first step can be taken . . . and then a whole lifetime of growth be supported."[33]

Perhaps the coercion related to altar time would cease if leaders began to look at salvation in the lives of children as more of a process than a singular crisis decision. Various decision points will mark this process as a child grows in his cognitive ability to grasp abstract concepts like love and eternity. Lois Lebar writes,

31 Tony Kummer, "Childhood Conversion and Age of Accountability" http://tonykummer. wordpress.com/2005/11/25/childhood-conversion-and-age-of-accountability-part-1-introduction/ (accessed June 2, 2008).

32 Richards, *Children's Ministry,* 375.

33 Ibid., 376.

If we provide small children frequent opportunities to say, "yes" to Christ in accordance with their limited comprehension of Him, we shall never err by hindering them from coming to the Savior, nor by being responsible for their making a mere profession before the Spirit has prepared the heart. We shall never be guilty of going to either extreme if we give our groups of children numerous occasions to confess their love of Christ, and then deal individually with those who seek salvation, a miracle which happens once for all time and eternity.[34]

Sometime in childhood, blessed by consistent exposure to the Christian message, the child will experience this once-and-for-all miracle. It may be at an altar or on a playground. It may happen with adult supervision or not. My son Aaron announced one morning at breakfast that he had asked Jesus to come into his heart. It was his first "public" confession of faith, and I understood that at age four, he didn't comprehend the full implications of his announcement. But my wife and I encouraged him anyway. We continued to nurture his faith at home and through the church. He prayed at altars on many occasions through the childhood years. Each experience only served to solidify his spiritual commitment that began before that breakfast table pronouncement. Barna states, "Anyone who wishes to have significant influence on the development of a person's moral and spiritual foundations had better exert that influence while the person is still open-minded and impressionable—in other words, while the person is still young."[35]

---

34 Lois E. Lebar, *Children in the Bible School* (Old Tappan, NJ: Fleming H. Revell Company, 1952), 171.

35 George Barna, *Transforming Children into Spiritual Champions* (Ventura: Regal Books, 2003), 47.

What Barna and I are explaining here is a process of letting children come to Jesus. Many times the methods used in formal children's ministry settings can limit a child's true response to the gospel. This occurs anytime the child is put in a position of feeling that he must respond in order to please a teacher. Hayes writes, "All of this discussion is meant to demonstrate the fact that when we seek to integrate a doctrine of salvation with a behavioral concept of evangelistic methodology, we encounter difficulty."[36] Our particular behavioral concept of evangelistic methodology may then be responsible for causing difficulty in producing a clearly authentic faith response in young children.

Our ethical response to the possibility that this is true must be to step back and assess the dynamics of what we are doing. We cannot continue with business as usual if that form of business is offending little ones. Jesus said, "And whoever welcomes one such child in my name welcomes me. If anyone causes one of these little ones—those who believe in me—to stumble, it would be better for them to have a large millstone hung around their neck and to be drowned in the depths of the sea."[37] Our ethical response is to adjust what we are doing so that children will be welcomed to Jesus without offense.

Conclusion

Edward Hayes wrote, "Giving an invitation is a natural and normal part of the gospel presentation. How it is done is quite another thing. Teachers are wise not to force or push for decisions. The gospel, rightly presented, has its own appeal. The Savior has His own drawing power. This is the divine work

---

36 Hayes, "Evangelism of Children," 257.
37 Matthew 18:5–6.

of the Holy Spirit in wedding human need and response to the winsomeness of Christ."[38] The children's worker in today's outreach setting must be willing to accept this "divine work of the Holy Spirit." Altar times cannot be forced, pressure-filled events in the lives of children.

In this chapter we began by looking at an ethical response to the age of accountability. This was followed by three segments addressing: (1) Faith or Fear; Setting aside scare tactics and letting God be God, (2) Pressure or Pleasure; Relaxing the altar time so that children can enjoy the presence of God, and (3) Let or Limit; Allowing children to come to Jesus rather than engaging in psycho-spiritual coercion.

Considering the length and depth of this work, all aspects of each segment allow for further study. Questions will continue to arise each time an altar call is given. Our "Christian" ethics, based in part on Christ's character, demand that we question, evaluate, and, if need be, adjust our approach when giving altar calls to children. In this world of confusion, foundations such as compassion, integrity, and faith continue to stand rock solid. While the storms of ego, impatience, and unbelief assail us, our godly ethics will stand. With the Lord's help, I believe that anyone involved in leading children to Christ can consider the arguments stated in this chapter and better serve the children and Jesus when altar time comes.

---

38 Hayes, "Evangelism of Children," 260.

SECTION 2—PRACTICAL IDEAS, PROGRAMS, AND APPLICATIONS

CHAPTER 6

THE IMPORTANCE OF PRAYER IN EVANGELISM

Introduction

Charles Spurgeon once wrote concerning reaching children, "Every real teacher's power must come from on high. If you never enter your closet and shut the door, if you never plead at the mercy seat for your child, how can you expect that God will honor you in its conversion?"[1] I believe this statement. Prayer on the part of the children's leader must predicate the genuine conversion of a child. You must be more than an entertainer; it is imperative that you become a person of prayer.

It has been my aim, by way of training and conviction, to include prayer in every aspect of evangelizing children. I have been a participant in children's crusades, special outreach events, and kids' camps, both as a leader and worker, since 1975. In that time, the success or failure of each opportunity has in many ways been related to the time spent in prayer both personally and corporately. I have witnessed thousands of children come

---

1   C. H. Spurgeon, *Come Ye Children* (Pasadena, TX: Pilgrim Publications, 1975), 154.

to altars across America and on several foreign fields. Prayer has always influenced the number of children responding and the intensity of that response.

Stanley Grenz writes, "Moral revival in a nation begins with the willingness of God's people to seek the face of God in prayer. God is the author of renewal, but in this task God wills the cooperation of human instruments, especially in prayer."[2] Moral revival cannot be limited to the adult believer. We have an opportunity to prayerfully influence the next generation for Christ. Yes, I am talking about a moral revival among our children. Through prayer the next political leaders, pastors, parents, and power brokers can be raised to know and to love the Lord Jesus.

I have witnessed no greater example of this than when serving during a short-term missions trip at The School of the Sword in Honduras in 1980. Pastor Don Hawks, the independent American missionary who founded and carved that school out of the jungle of this Latin American country, was a man of prayer.

Armed with prayer and sheer determination, Don opened this boarding school in the early 1960s. Boys could stay there up to seven or eight years, obtaining a sixth-grade education as well as learning a trade. At the time of my visit, 180 boys were current residents and thousands of boys had spent time as students at Pastor Don's school. I have been told that upon his death in the late 1980s, there were School of the Sword graduates in places of power and influence in many high-level government and industrial offices in the country. His funeral was a national event. His work to evangelize and train children, founded on prayer, was influencing the moral climate of an entire nation.

---

2   Stanley Grenz, *Prayer: A Cry For The Kingdom* (Peabody, MA: Hendrickson Publishers, 1988), 5.

Prayer must play a vital role in the life and ministry of the children's leader. It is only prayer that will allow the leader to have an eternal effect on children, families, communities, and nations. This aspect of ministerial life is more important than learning to operate a puppet or give an altar call. Prayer must take priority over slick advertisements, big banana splits, and visitor contest giveaways.

The first portion of this chapter will deal with the personal prayer life of the children's leader. In this section I will examine my life and ministry as it relates to prayer and the children's leader. Application for your life and ministry will be made as I explore each of the following four areas: My Journey, Personal Devotions and Prayer, Prayer in the Leader's Family, and Corporate Prayer. After this, I will take a look at the importance of prayer when evangelizing children. I will break this down into three important segments: Background Thoughts, Bringing Prayer into the Pulpit, and Believing in Prayer and the Altar Service.

Dutch Sheets, in his book, *Intercessory Prayer*, encourages the Christian worker, saying, "The most important point I want to communicate to you through this book is that God wants to use you."[3] I echo this in saying that the most important thing I want to communicate to you through this chapter is that God wants to use you. He wants to use you to bring His life-changing power into the trenches of child evangelism. He wants to use you in power-packed altar services as you allow boys and girls to come to Jesus. As you read this "prayer chapter," consider for a moment that the prayer chapter of

---

3   Dutch Sheets, *Intercessory Prayer* (Ventura, CA: Regal Books, 1996), 105.

your life and ministry is just beginning to be written. There is great potential in you, the children's leader, if you will only give yourself to God in prayer and act according to His divine directives.

My Journey

I was saved in a kitchen in south Omaha on January 19, 1975. In that same kitchen, a little grandmother laid her hand on my shoulder and said, "Don't be afraid, just raise your hands and praise the Lord." I did, and Holy Spirit filled me to overflowing. I began to speak with other tongues as the Spirit enabled me. In the few moments it took me to step into a kitchen and receive from God, my prayer life shot from nonexistent lethargy to energized continuity. Prayer became a newfound priority in my life.

God seems to take pleasure in trusting me to tackle tasks that seem too great for me to handle alone. Soon after I was born again, my fiancée, Darlene, and I began assisting with bus ministry. We were bus captains with a great deal of zeal and no training or experience. So we were driven to pray.

It wasn't long before I was helping with crowd control in children's church. Eventually the leader let me present an occasional lesson or puppet show from the front of the room. This was scary and wonderful all at once. I still had no training, but I loved God and loved the kids. I was driven to pray.

Our first kids' crusade[4] was a total faith experience. If you measured the success of it by the world's standards it was doomed from the start. Darlene and I packed our toddler, Sarah, into the

---

4   A "kids' crusade" was a three-to-five-day event held in a church during the course of a week. Each evening of the crusade, children were challenged by an evangelist to put their faith and trust in Jesus. Puppets, songs, stories, and prizes were common in these congregational outreaches to children. These crusades have a rich history and only began to fade out in the 1980s and early 1990s.

car and drove from Minneapolis, Minnesota, to Tell City, Indiana. We left with enough money to get to the final destination, ministered to a handful of children all week, and returned home with nothing but memories to show for our week. We had never preached a kids' crusade and barely had enough material to fill the time each evening. So we were driven to pray.

Dan Crawford writes, "Could it be that God desires to have fellowship with us and that our need to commune with God is a result of God's greater need to commune with us? Could it be that God shaped us for this very purpose?"[5] If God has indeed shaped us for the purpose of communing with Him, then all we do in ministry is designed to steer us back to that course of action. I think we reverse God's plan by seeing prayer as a support for ministry when in reality, God designed ministry to be a support for prayer.

I once walked down a spiral staircase in a restored Victorian mansion. As I descended the stairs into the main foyer, each step was wider than the last. Ministry has been this way for me. Every step I take has increased or widened the need in me to spend more time in prayer. It seems like each task God calls me to is impossible. Children are under attack, and to run interference between them and the attacker is impossible by human standards.

I like what Dutch Sheets writes: "Jack Hayford says, 'But there is a way to face impossibility. Invade it! Not with glib speech of high hopes. Not in anger. Not with resignation. Not through stoical self-control. But with violence. And prayer provides the vehicle for this kind of violence.'"[6] God, let me become violent in my relentless prayer attack on those forces that would seek to destroy childhood.

---

5   Dan Crawford, *The Prayer-Shaped Disciple* (Peabody, MA: Hendrickson Publishers, 1999), xiv.

6   Sheets, *Intercessory Prayer*, 138.

I must admit, in my early ministry, my prayer was driven by crisis management. God placed the next bigger-than-me crisis, challenge, or ministry in my path and I would pray until I could get through it. Times have changed me, and my approach to prayer. I have learned by practice to pray before crisis occurs. Prayer has become an all-day, every-day practice.

Ed Silvoso once quoted a poll indicating that "95% of Americans have had at least one prayer answered."[7] I have had many prayers answered in a positive way over the years. I once led a children's service during which prayer was offered on behalf of one of our church's ten-year-olds. She had fallen the day before and was hospitalized in critical condition. We all prayed together and God healed her.

God hasn't always said "yes" to me. Some prayers have reaped no healing or desired result. It seems like a large amount of my prayers are answered in the "wait a while" manner.

I have been taught over the years that God answers prayer with yes, no, or wait. Dan Crawford says, "Furthermore, I think God's answer is occasionally we'll see."[8] This answer reveals a loving Father image. "The next time you feel God has answered with a we'll see, allow him the privilege of being sovereign and having a change of mind without being inconsistent."[9]

Being raised in a broken home, with my father absent during my teen years, the concept of a heavenly Father who loves and listens to me took some getting used to after my conversion. "We call not on a father who is preoccupied with his career and has little time for his children. We call not on a father who may find someone else he loves more and so forsake

---

7   Ed Silvoso, *That None Should Perish* (Ventura, CA: Regal Books, 1994), 76.

8   Crawford, *The Prayer-Shaped Disciple*, 36.

9   Ibid., 37.

us. Nor does the father on whom we call simply cater to our whims while we manipulate him."[10] I have learned over the years that my heavenly Father will direct my life and ministry. He does this in such a way that I am compelled to spend optimum time with Him each day. This time is found early in the morning as I begin the day with Him. Like Brother Lawrence[11] of old, I do my best to practice His presence by praying all through the day.

"John Wesley spent two hours daily in prayer beginning at four in the morning, and Martin Luther said, 'If I fail to spend two hours in prayer each morning, the devil gets the victory through the day.' . . . We usually work our prayer times around our personal schedule. Jesus, on the other hand, worked his schedule around his prayer life."[12] I strive personally to work my schedule around my prayer life. When I get this priority backwards, God's sweet Holy Spirit gently draws me closer and reminds me to put Jesus first.

Personal Devotions and Prayer

When I was first saved, an older Christian brother said to me, "A Proverb a day keeps the devil away." This brother encouraged me to read a chapter from Proverbs each day. Although this has not kept the devil away, it has provided me with some terrific devotional times over the years. I continue to read that chapter of Proverbs that coincides with the calendar date. I also follow my wife's example of reading through the Bible each year. But devotions are more than just reading the Bible.

---

10 Ibid., 5.

11 Brother Lawrence was a monk who whose writings have been compiled in a work entitled, "Practicing The Presence." His work encourages an all-day-long experience with God.

12 Crawford, *The Prayer-Shaped Disciple*, 106–107.

"Charles Spurgeon once said, 'Let us meet and pray, and if God doth not hear us, it will be the first time He has broken His promise.'"[13] God wants to commune with us in prayer. Stanley Grenz writes, "Gypsy Smith said, 'Get down on your knees and confess all known sin. Determine to follow the Lord wherever His Word directs you no matter what the cost. Ask Him to begin His work in you! When this prayer is answered, you will have the beginning of a revival in your church.'"[14] If I want to see revival in my public ministry, then my life must, in private, be dedicated to God in prayer. I am constantly asking God to begin a new work in me.

I need no urging to spend time alone with my wife, Darlene. I love her and relish the opportunities we have each day to speak with and to see each other. She listens to me and I to her. Why should it be so difficult to do the same with Jesus?

"Because it is just you alone, there are self-restraints required in private prayer. You will not have the support of another Christian or group of Christians to hold you accountable to the task of praying."[15] I have had marvelous times alone with God. At other times, I have wondered if God was even near me. The discipline of private or personal devotions should not be dependent on feelings. Self-discipline or self-restraint must rule the day. My friend George Edgerly used to say, "We are to worship Him in spirit and in truth. In spirit when we feel like it and in truth when we don't."

The first lead pastor I served with, Jerry Strandquist, encouraged personal devotions. He required that the staff read books on prayer and devotions. He quizzed us on Bible verses we were

---

13 Ibid., 83–84

14 Grenz, *Prayer: A Cry*, 5.

15 Crawford, *The Prayer-Shaped Disciple*, 54.

to memorize in personal devotions. He took us to seminars on prayer. We even hosted some of these at our church. He enrolled me in the Change the World School of Prayer seminar. Our staff then met together at regular times to share and to pray. These personal devotional and staff prayer times are my best memories of my first children's pastorate. I thank God that I had that kind of relational discipleship prayer training in my first years of full-time ministry.

I once had a children's pastor call me to complain that his pastor wanted to join him and other staff members at 7:00 each morning to pray. This young minister was indignant. He couldn't believe that pastor had the nerve to require this kind of accountability. I encouraged him to praise God for a pastor that cared enough to pray, to encourage him to pray, and to model a prayer lifestyle that involved the staff.

I find that regular study for my sermons, camps, teachings, or other meetings is not enough to fill my spirit. I must spend time with Jesus! Devotion must be more than a catchphrase for Christian living. The term *devotion* implies a decision for continued commitment to Christ. I am devoted to my Savior.

Dan Crawford provides a great list of reasons for personal prayer time. He writes, "Why spend time in private prayer?

- ❑ The more time we spend with someone, the better acquainted we become.
- ❑ Extended time in prayer affords you ample opportunity for personal renewal and reflection.
- ❑ It will allow greater time of intercession for others.
- ❑ It offers deeper preparation for service."[16]

---

16 Ibid., 58.

So I spend time in prayer personally. You, as a children's leader, must spend personal time in prayer and devotion. God must first have His way in your heart if you are to have any eternal effect on the hearts and lives of children.

What is personal prayer? I like Stanley Grenz's definition: "In short, prayer is a crying to God for help based on an awareness of dependence on God."[17] I believe in God, therefore I cry out to Him and listen for an answer. Prayer is a time when I can speak to my Father and He can speak to me. "The greatest thing anyone can do for God and for man is to pray. It is not the only thing. It is the chief thing."[18]

If prayer is indeed that chief thing that we can do as individual believers, then we should be sold out and radical in this aspect of Christian living. I find this next statement to be incredibly freeing: "Prayer is perhaps the only task of the church in which every Christian can participate. One does not need special status, financial resources, or flashy spiritual gifts to be involved in this ministry. Any Christian can become a giant of prayer."[19] While I continue to sharpen my abilities for ministry, I am not bound by lack of experience or skill. I can reach children for Jesus through faithful devotion and prayer followed by God-directed and empowered action. As I spend time with Jesus, the lover of children, I will naturally grow in my Christlike compassion for children.

The children's leader must become a person of prayer. Evangelizing children is of primary importance to the life of the church of today and the future. This task cannot be built on the shaky foundation of human understanding and talents. It

---

17 Grenz, *Prayer: A Cry*, 40.

18 Ibid., 6.

19 Ibid., 5.

must be founded on prayer, established in prayer, and grown through prayer. Don Crawford writes, "I've found the best way to minister in the midst of a group of people is to spend some time alone with God."[20] Stanley Grenz writes that personal prayer includes three things.

- ❑ Personal prayer includes meditation.
- ❑ Personal prayer is verbalized prayer.
- ❑ Personal prayer includes times of silence.[21]

My personal strategy in this matter includes the ACTS model: Adoration, Confession, Thanksgiving, and Supplication. This is a model discussed in many books on prayer, and I use it because it is easy to remember.

Adoration is time spent praising and adoring God. I don't do this because of what He's done, but because of who He is. How easy it is to enter into a right attitude in prayer while adoring my Maker. My friend Paul Grabill said, "We may not realize how personal our personal God is." Adoration is a personal act directed towards a personal God.

Confession is a time of personal cleansing. I ask God to take away my sin. I pray the Lord's Prayer during this time. I ask God to forgive my debts as I forgive the debts of others. I lay my thoughts, actions, and words on the altar of forgiveness. In doing this, I am made aware once again of my insignificance and His greatness. Confession is an act of humility. James 4:6 says, "But he gives us more grace. That is why Scripture says: 'God opposes the proud but shows favor to the humble.'"

---

20 Crawford, *The Prayer-Shaped Disciple*, 98.
21 Grenz, *Prayer: A Cry*, 95.

Thanksgiving is my favorite time in prayer. Stanley Grenz writes, "Thanksgiving is the natural outgrowth of confession."[22] I cannot thank God enough for the wonderful things He has done for me and for my family. Every day there are new blessings. This is a time of remembrance and blessing. God is good all the time!

Supplication is the time when I make requests of God. I must admit that when I pray with my children before bedtime, supplication seems to be the order of the day. We pray for our pastors and missionaries and loved ones far off. In the ACTS model, supplication is the final quarter of our prayer time. In practice it can easily become the one and only prayer act. I encourage you to adopt the ACTS model in your private prayer times. Expand your prayer time beyond supplication to include adoration, confession, and thanksgiving.

Pastor Grabill refers to the Lord's Prayer as "The Disciples Prayer." It provides a model for extended personal prayer times. Read it now from Matthew 6:9–13.

> Our Father in heaven, hallowed be your name, your kingdom come, your will be done, on earth as it is in heaven. Give us today our daily bread. And forgive us our debts, as we also have forgiven our debtors. And lead us not into temptation, but deliver us from the evil one.

The following list of "P" words summarizing the Lord's Prayer was shared by Pastor Grabill in a prayer seminar in the summer of 2002.

Praise/Adoration—"our Father"—This is the time of worshipping God.

---

22 Ibid., 21.

Partner—"thy kingdom come, thy will be done"—In this portion of prayer I bring to God those important issues which are on my heart while I pray.

Provision—"daily bread"—This includes any physical concerns I have for myself or my family.

Pardon/Grace—"forgive as we forgive"—I now become active in forgiving others and seeking God's forgiveness.

Providence—"lead us"—The concerns of following God's will can consume this portion of the prayer time. I like to include a cry for more of His power, holiness, and Spirit.

Protection—"deliver us from evil"—The final segment is committed to prayer for protection and overcoming power.

Some days I pray one way and others another. Whatever pattern you choose to follow, make it a point to pray! Guard your schedule, allowing prayer to become the priority in your life and ministry. "We become so busy for Him, we don't have time to be with Him. We're dragging our ministry around in circles, going nowhere and accomplishing nothing for the kingdom of God."[23]

Prayer in the Leader's Family

Ed Silvoso discusses the devastating effect of spiritual strongholds on the pastor and his family. The enemy of our souls is working overtime to rip apart pastors and their wives and children. He says, "How can they [pastors] believe God for a miracle for their cities if they find themselves unable to enjoy their marriages or forgive someone who has hurt them or to believe God for a breakthrough in their local congregation?"[24] Prayer must be an important part of ministerial family life.

---

23 Sheets, *Intercessory Prayer*, 145.
24 Ed Silvoso, *That None Should Perish*, 157.

Prayer has been an everyday practice in our home. My wife is an incredible woman of prayer. Her example has done much to train our children. I have also attempted to model for our children a lifestyle of constant communion with the heavenly Father. This has included prayer in every arena of life. It is not unusual for any member of our family to blurt out, "My Father made that," whenever we pass a tree, sunset, or colorful bird. We remind each other often and in every situation that God is present.

Dutch Sheets writes, "I think Christ is awesome and wants us to be awesomites. Humble awesomites representing His awesomeness, but awesome nonetheless."[25] The children's leader must become an awesomite first in his family and then in the pulpit. I do not believe that the children's leader can maintain an awesomite ministry in public if a lifestyle of prayer is nonexistent in the privacy of his own family. Let me mention here that my standard of raising my children as awesomites has never been dependent on the opinion of others. My children need to know that I am their biggest fan and God is cheering them on. They will learn awesomite Christian living by my example.

Don Crawford writes about teaching your children to pray. This is a daunting task for the normal parent. Add the daily stress of ministry to the mix and the task can seem insurmountable. How do I teach my own children to pray? Crawford gives this list of guidelines for this holy endeavor:

Suggestions in helping children learn how to pray:

1. Set an example.
2. Never criticize your children's prayers.
3. Never insist that your children pray aloud.

---

25 Sheets, *Intercessory Prayer*, 45.

4. Use conversational prayer.

5. Vary body positions as you pray.

6. Use lists and pictures.

7. Teach them to pray big to increase their faith.

8. Teach your children to trust God.[26]

It has been our practice to set aside time for prayer each evening before bed. While our children grew we prayed with them about daily concerns. We'd then pray for our pastors, church leadership, and for specific missionaries. Through these times, our children grew up loving the ministry and missionaries. I believe much of the respect they have for me and for my wife is a direct result of our honoring God's authorities in our times of prayer.

The children's leader/pastor must develop a strategy for prayer in the home. Ours included the bedtime prayer as I have mentioned, but also included prayer for any given ministry or need at any given time of the day. I have often prayed with my children while driving them to and from school. My son Tim and I began this when he was in kindergarten. Over the years we prayed about everything in life during those rides in the car. He is a youth and media pastor today.

The family unit is the ultimate small group prayer circle. When agreeing to pray for someone on a regular basis, Crawford writes, "It is simple in that it is easy to agree to share your prayer needs with one other person or to pray for the needs of another person. It is complex in that it requires time, discipline, concern, and sensitivity."[27] The advantage of praying in the family unit is that concern and sensitivity are in place naturally. You only need concern yourself with setting a regular time to pray with

---

26 Crawford, *The Prayer-Shaped Disciple,* 21.

27 Ibid., 17.

and for one another. It then becomes a matter of maintaining the discipline necessary to make prayer time a family habit.

Stanley Grenz writes, "Many Christians do not pray because they are not convinced that prayer works; they do not understand what prayer is, how prayer functions, or for what they should pray."[28] I propose to you that in order to raise up a generation of believers, you must insist on having family prayer, and that family prayer must be offered with an assurance that God will hear and answer. With young children, there is no room for doubt. They have great faith. We, as parents, must become as our own children in the theology of prayer.

Effective evangelism of children is an outgrowth of the quality of prayer in the children's leader's family. Prayer with and for your family will strengthen your ministry to other families. Establish a prayer time and pattern. Maintain the discipline of that family altar, and pray with assurance that God loves each one of you. He wants to answer your prayers.

Corporate Prayer

Can you picture your city from God's perspective? Try to imagine it as God sees it. A city enveloped in thick spiritual darkness. . . . Now watch the sum of believers piercing that shield of darkness by lifting up holy hands in which they carry the names and the needs of all the inhabitants of the city. Satan cannot stop them because his only active weapon is sin, and they have clothed themselves in holiness. Day and night the names of each one of the inhabitants is presented before God. What a turnaround for the church.[29]

---

28 Grenz, *Prayer: A Cry*, 47.

29 Ed Silvoso, *That None Should Perish*, 90.

Ed Silvoso paints a picture here of what can be in any city on planet earth. Imagine now this principle at work in your life. What would happen in an outreach if you mobilized your church and others in community prayer?

Let me take this a step closer to home. Replace the word "city" in the above paragraph with the word "ministry."

Can you picture your *children's ministry* from God's perspective? Try to imagine it as God sees it. A *children's ministry* enveloped in thick spiritual darkness. . . . Now watch the sum of believers piercing that shield of darkness by lifting up holy hands in which they carry the names and the needs of *you and your ministry to children*. Satan cannot stop them because his only active weapon is sin, and they have clothed themselves in holiness. Day and night the names of each one is presented before God. What a turnaround for the *children's ministry*.

Imagine with me what would happen if a children's leader engaged in ministry where believers were in prayer for the lost as well as for the leader and his family. What kind of outreach results could be expected if such a prayer force were summoned?

The children's leader of tomorrow must become a person of prayer who depends on the corporate strength of many believers praying and standing behind his ministry. He must hold himself responsible for the spiritual growth of his own family. Growing from this is his responsibility for the spiritual rebirth and growth of others and their children. Henri Nouwen writes, "In our world of loneliness and despair, there is an enormous need for men and women who know the heart of God, a heart that forgives, cares, reaches out and wants to heal."[30]

---

30 Henri Nouwen, *In the Name of Jesus: Reflections on Christian Leadership.* (New York: Crossroad, 1989), 37.

The children's leader must come into an understanding of the corporate plan of Christ for any ministry. He will not survive without the support and prayers of other believers. Dutch Sheets develops a compelling argument for the cooperative aspect of any ministry or ministry leader. God's ministries are under siege by an enemy who understands our humanity. Sheets urges believers to stand behind pastors and other church leaders. He offers,

Here are five reasons pastors and other church leaders are in such great need of watchmen (alert prayer warriors) interceding for them:

1. Pastors have more responsibility and accountability.
2. Pastors are more subject to temptation.
3. Pastors are more targeted by spiritual warfare.
4. Pastors have more influence on others.
5. Pastors have more visibility.[31]

There is freedom in acknowledging your dependence on the body of Christ. You need the body and the body needs you. Part of your prayer approach should be to find faithful men and women who will join with you on a daily basis, wherever you are, and lift your family and ministry before God in prayer.

"Every minister needs a prayer team, covering him or her with intercession. One survey taken among pastors revealed 33% of them saying, 'Being in the ministry is clearly a hazard to my family.' Likewise, 33% felt burnout within the first five years of ministry."[32]

Have you found yourself feeling burnout? Have you ever ended a four-day outreach and wished you could go sell used cars? You need a prayer team! You need friends whom you can

---

31 Sheets, *Intercessory Prayer*, 246.

32 Crawford, *The Prayer-Shaped Disciple*, 86–87.

call on any time of the day or night for corporate, "two or more gathered in His name" prayer.

Charles Spurgeon once wrote, "May you strive for the grandest of all ends, the salvation of immortal souls. Your business is not merely to teach children to read the Bible, not barely to inculcate the duties of morality, nor even to instruct them in the mere letter of the gospel, but your high calling is to be the means, in the hands of God, of bringing life from heaven to dead souls."[33]

I submit that if you develop a growing personal, family, and corporate prayer strategy, you will fulfill your high calling. Your ministry will move from simply entertaining and teaching Bible stories to becoming the means, in the hands of God, of bringing life from heaven to hell-bound souls of every age.

---

33 C. H. Spurgeon, *Come Ye Children* (Pasadena, TX: Pilgrim Publications, 1975), 149.

CHAPTER 7

THE IMPORTANCE OF PRAYER WHEN EVANGELIZING CHILDREN

Background Thoughts

In 1948, Frank Coleman wrote, "No child should be left to grow up in our world of unbelief and flagrant sin without his having heard the Gospel with persuasive invitation to believe it and accept its salvation."[1]

Although praying for and working toward the salvation of the lost is as old as the church, the practice of doing these things on behalf of children is relatively new.

The year is 1780, the place, England. "Robert Raikes fails miserably when trying to reach and reform prisoners. He decides to go after the children so that they may grow up to become good citizens. With the children working in factories six days a week the only time he could teach them was on Sunday. He hired a teacher, paid children a penny to come to 'Sunday School,' and began teaching them the basics of reading, writing, and morals using the Bible as a text."[2]

---

1 Frank G. Coleman, *The Romance of Winning Children* (Cleveland: Union Gospel Press, 1948), 9.

2 Wayne Widder, "Reviewing Historical Foundations," in *Christian Education: Founda-*

This is one of the first modern references to somebody attempting to formally reach numbers of children with the gospel. Since 1780, God has raised up new ideas and well-equipped armies of people to reach boys and girls for His kingdom. Only prayer could bring about success in these endeavors.

What about prayer in general? "Prayer is present among all societies and all peoples in the world. This has led some to conclude that prayer is natural, rooted in the instinctive recognition of one's dependence on a higher power."[3] Whether or not that statement is true can be debated by those far more knowledgeable than I. I believe that as long as there has been prayer, there have been parents praying for their children.

Jesus offered prayer on behalf of the children. In Matthew 19:13–15 we read, "Then people brought little children to Jesus for him to place his hands on them and pray for them. But the disciples rebuked them. Jesus said, 'Let the little children come to me, and do not hinder them, for the kingdom of heaven belongs to such as these.' When he had placed his hands on them, he went on from there." He sets an example here for the church of today. Children and children's evangelism need prayer.

In Scripture, we find that prayer was a normal part of everyday life. "The words chosen to refer to prayer were normal, secular words."[4] People in Jesus' time prayed. The church should take note that people in Jesus' day also believed that God would bless children through the prayers of His teachers or prophets. We should then take note that Jesus did not discourage this

---

tions for the Future, Ed. by Robert Clark, Lin Johnson, and Allyn K. Sloat (Chicago: Moody Press, 1991), 53.

3   Grenz, Prayer: A Cry, 7.

4   Ibid., 18.

belief. He took the time to place His hands on them and pray for them. But Jesus did more than that. He encouraged the people of His day, and the church throughout the generations to follow, to pray for children. He tells us to "Let the little children come to me, and do not hinder them." We know that children can and will come to Jesus.

"Call the roll of the saints of God who have led the forces of the church, who have pioneered in world missions, who have taught the people of God. The vast majority of them were saved in childhood days."[5] So child evangelism, whether by plan or default, has influenced the church of Jesus Christ throughout the ages. Prayer is a catalyst for this movement.

"There is no larger soul value in the world than children. To impress boys and girls themselves with the value of giving their whole lives to Jesus, we sometimes ask them if they would keep an apple and not eat it until it has rotted, or an ice cream cone until it melts, or a new pair of shoes until they are too small, or an automobile until it is rusted."[6] This is as true today as it was when Lois Lebar wrote it in 1952. Children need the Lord. Prayer must be offered on their behalf if they are to have a genuine, life-changing experience.

Prayer, or petition made on behalf of children, is an act willed by God himself. "Petition is the laying hold of and the releasing of God's willingness and ability to act in accordance with God's will and purpose on behalf of creation that God loves."[7] It is God's will that "all" will come to a saving knowledge of Him. God has made it clear that He desires children to be part of

---

5   Coleman, *The Romance*, 10.

6   Lois E. Lebar, *Children in the Bible School* (Old Tappan, NJ: Fleming H. Revell Company, 1952), 27.

7   Grenz, *Prayer: A Cry*, 39.

that "all." So prayer or petition on the part of children and for the salvation of children is in keeping with God's will.

"D. L. Moody said, 'We are to ask with a beggar's humility, to seek with a servant's carefulness, and to knock with the confidence of a friend.'"[8] As children's leaders, we are to do this on behalf of the children. We must allow the Holy Spirit to impart in us a passion for the lost boys and girls of planet Earth. That passion will then fuel a continuous asking, seeking, and knocking that will bring results in the salvation of children everywhere.

Bringing Prayer into the Pulpit

Why should prayer be such a big part of what we do in the evangelism of children? A simple answer can be found in Dan Crawford's writings: "A Christian should pray because the Bible teaches prayer."[9] Crawford goes on to give us specific reasons to pray.

- We might delight God.
- We will not lose heart.
- We might be strengthened.
- We may be healed.
- We might increase our wisdom.
- The peace of God will guard our hearts and minds.
- We will find compassion.
- We may make known with boldness the mystery of the gospel.[10]

Each one of these reasons is complementary to reaching children. *We pray so that we might delight God.* What better

---

8   Crawford, *The Prayer-Shaped Disciple*, 118.

9   Ibid., 111.

10   Ibid., 112.

reason do we have to communicate with our Maker? We must delight Him and take delight in communing with Him.

We pray so that we will not lose heart. We live in a day and age when the forces of evil have drawn battle lines. We must do all we can to combat the temptation to become weary in well doing.

We pray that we might be strengthened. The children's leader needs the strength and power of the Holy Spirit. Each year I find it a little bit harder to kneel down behind that puppet stage, to stay up late with the kids at camp, or to maintain high energy levels during meetings. I need God's strength.

We pray so that we may be healed. Children's evangelism must continue and grow in the future. The children's leader must be a well-oiled tool ready to be used in the Master's hand. Healing is paramount to this occurring.

We pray for an increase in our wisdom. Each week I come across another question or shocking situation that requires my input or assistance. Each time this happens, I turn to God for His wisdom and understanding. James 1:5 states, "If any of you lacks wisdom, you should ask God, who gives generously to all without finding fault, and it will be given to you." The prayer for wisdom should be a daily part of the children's leader's prayer regimen.

We pray that the peace of Christ will guard our hearts and minds. I don't know if you have noticed, but the world can be confusing. The enemy—the author of confusion—is at work. The peace of Christ is a protection needed by the children's leader. I once had an evangelist come to my church. He arrived for the children's outreach with an attitude. He had been mistreated the week prior to our event and was determined to take this out on us. He lost, we lost, and the children lost. If only this brother had allowed the peace of Christ to guard his heart, we would all have had a different experience that week.

We pray so that we may grow in compassion. We need Christ-like compassion for the children and families we are serving. I pray that God will give me the same compassion for the foul-mouthed, dirty-nosed, head lice-ridden bus kid as He does for the pretty little deacon's daughter who does everything right.

We pray that we may make known with boldness the mystery of the gospel. If ever there was a time to preach the Word with boldness, it is now. Children need more than flannelgraphs, puppets, PowerPoint, and slick tricks. They need the life-saving power of Jesus Christ.

Prayer, then, must become part of your plan for child evangelism. From the first letter to the host church, you must emphasize the need for prayer. Encourage people young and old to pray for the crusade, camp, or special event. I am going to speak at a church later this summer that has been having prayer meetings on behalf of the crusade since January. I can hardly wait to see what God will do in the lives of children at this praying church.

Being the children's leader affords you the opportunity to pray in public. Stanley Grenz gives us guidelines to follow when praying publicly. He suggests:

1. The one who prays publicly must be sensitive to the leading of the Spirit.
2. Remember that prayer is being addressed to God by a representative of the people, and not to the people by the representative of God.
3. Be sensitive to prayer length and volume.
4. Live a lifestyle worthy of the honor of praying in public.[11]

Let's look in more detail at the guidelines mentioned above.

---

11 Grenz, *Prayer: A Cry*, 103–104.

The one who prays publicly must be sensitive to the leading of the Spirit. Whether it is the opening prayer at a kids' crusade or the closing prayer of a camp altar service, the children's leader must be in tune with the Holy Spirit. Frank Coleman writes, "A great many Christians regard the *reaching* of children as a highly specialized ministry, demanding the services of a 'children's expert.' The simple truth is that any yielded saint can be an effective soul winner among boys and girls if he will take God's way."[12] In praying publicly and in ministry to children, become a willing vessel. Yield your life, thoughts, words, and actions to the Holy Spirit.

Remember that *prayer is being addressed to God by a representative of the people, and not to the people by the representative of God.* Do not get caught up in your own ability to deliver a fine sentence. You are talking to God on behalf of the children. The adults may pay attention to what you say, but the boys and girls will pay attention to who you are. Your prayers in front of a group of children must be sincere, joy filled, and spoken from the heart. You are addressing God on behalf of one of His favorite people groups.

Be sensitive to prayer length and volume. The wise children's leader knows when to be quiet. Keep it short, saint. I have witnessed children's leaders frightening boys and girls with great volume or speed during their prayers. I like to approach the verbal speed and volume of Fred Rogers when I pray publicly with children. I want the boys and girls to approach God with confidence. Great volume does not impress children, nor do I think it impresses God.

---

12 Coleman, *The Romance*, 23.

Live a lifestyle worthy of the honor of praying in public. Being called a leader is not an automatic guarantee that a person is living for God. It is important that the leader live a life worthy of his calling. Children can spot a phony. Often the honor of praying in public is assumed by the leader whether he deserves it or not. Determine to become deserving in your life, attitudes, and speech.

I once attended a children's outreach during which the leader went right from the opening song into his program and never led the kids in prayer until altar time an hour and a half later. Prayer is the needed transition between opening thoughts and the body of your message. We must model dependency on God by praying first thing in every service. I would never think of beginning an outreach service without first praying. I pray aloud that God would bless the service—that He would give the children self-control in great abundance, and that He would give us good response at the altar.

Believing in Prayer and the Altar Service

If we provide small children frequent opportunities to say "yes" to Christ in accordance with their limited comprehension of Him, we shall never err by hindering them from coming to the Savior, nor by being responsible for their making a mere profession before the Spirit has prepared the heart.[13]

The altar call or altar service is just such an opportunity. Children are allowed to respond. They are given the opportunity to say yes to Jesus. This can be a very meaningful and precious

13 Lebar, *Children in the Bible School*, 171.

time. It is certainly the one point in any children's service that should be bathed in prayer.

"The real challenge in ministry with boys and girls is to provide that context in which the first step can be taken . . . and then a whole lifetime of growth be supported."[14] The camp, service, or special evangelism event are perfect forums for the taking of this first step.

Dutch Sheets says, "Smear everything your children have with the anointing!"[15] I add to that, "smear everything you do with and for children with the anointing." Altar service should be totally smeared or immersed in the anointing of God. That doesn't happen by wishing or by programming, it happens by prayer.

Many children's leaders are guilty of assuming that if the Word is preached in its various child-friendly forms, then God will simply show up at the altar call. They think that this will happen whether we have invited Him or not. I say, "No way!" Prayer for the anointing of God's Holy Spirit must be offered for every portion of the children's service.

The altar call is oftentimes called the "invitation." We call it that because it is a time of inviting children to respond to God's calling. We must realize that to invite the children to respond without the Holy Spirit of God is to give invitation to failure.

Praying for an effective, life-altering altar call is mandatory in reaching children today. We must experience the presence of God as He changes the hearts of boys and girls. Praying for this kind of altar time demands that the children's leader pray for the lost

---

14 Lawrence O. Richards, *Children's Ministry* (Grand Rapids: Zondervan Publishing, 1983), 374.

15 Sheets, *Intercessory Prayer*, 211.

children He is working to reach. This in turn demands that the leader believe the children need a Savior. Acknowledging this need will drive the leader to pray and prepare with a newfound passion.

"I am not talking about having a keen interest in the salvation of sinners. No! I am talking about an all-consuming passion for the lost ones. . . . I am talking about a lifestyle through which we devote every ounce of our energy to reaching the lost. If you lack this kind of passion, do not be discouraged. This is not something with which we are born, nor something that can be learned. It can neither be bought nor taught. It has to be imparted by the Holy Spirit."[16]

Do you have an all-consuming passion for the lost ones? Do you even believe that children can be lost ones? It is this belief that compels me to reach the children. If there is the chance that one child may die and spend eternity without Christ, it is my duty to do all I can to win them. Prayer is the one constant factor in the successful evangelism of people of any age.

"Throughout church history an awakening to prayer among the people of God has constituted the key to church renewal. Every spiritual awakening of significance from the beginning of Acts to the Welsh revival early in this century had its roots in prayer."[17] If there is to be a spiritual awakening among children, there must be prayer.

The key tool in building better altar services is prayer. Eternal work will be done in the hearts and minds of children when the leader sharpens his tools through prayer.

Children love to respond at the altars. It can become easy for the children's leader to become complacent in this area of praying for the altar service because boys and girls will respond.

---

16 Silvoso, *That None Should Perish,* 92.

17 Grenz, *Prayer: A Cry,* 4.

Let us look at the common salvation altar call given in a children's crusade service. The leader has every child close his eyes and think about Jesus. After summarizing what he taught all evening, the leader asks for a show of hands from the children who wish to respond. He invites those who have raised their hands to come to the altar for prayer. Children respond and the altar fills.

Kids come down to the altar for a variety of reasons. Some come because they want to be where the action is. They see others coming down and get excited. It is the first time in ninety minutes that the adults have allowed the children to leave their seats, so the child goes forward. That same child may be coming down to be near the leader.

Another child feels the presence of God and doesn't know what to do. He has already given his life to Christ, but is directed by the leader to come forward. So in an effort to please God, whose presence he feels, and to please the leader who is bringing everyone forward, the child takes those steps. Later, his parents cannot understand why he keeps responding to altar calls.

Yet another child has a felt need that he/she wishes to offer up in prayer. The leader brings these children down in the group not knowing that they do not want to be saved, they only want God to perform some miracle of help or healing.

Finally, there is that group of children who genuinely feel the need of a Savior and respond at the altar to give their lives to Him. These children live what Lois Lebar wrote about when she said, "Whereas many adults must be compelled to come to Christ, the children are eager to come if only we adults get out of their way and let them come."[18] These boys and girls want to come to Jesus if we will only get out of their way.

---

18 Lebar, *Children in the Bible School*, 20.

You can see by my writing that the children's leader must not only pray for a compassion for the lost child, but he must pray for discernment and wisdom in directing those children who respond to the altar call. Assisting children at the altar involves more than leading them in a canned prayer. It involves listening to the individual children and to the Holy Spirit of God, then praying accordingly.

Spurgeon once said,

> Your mouth must find out the child's words so that the child may know what you mean; you must feel a child's feelings, so as to be his companion and friend; you must be a student of juvenile sin; you must be a sympathizer in juvenile trials; you must, so far as possible, enter into childhood's joys and griefs. God will not raise a dead child by you if you are not willing to become all things to that child, if by any possibility you may win its soul.[19]

This kind of consecration on the part of the children's leader can only come from the Holy Spirit through a lifestyle of prayer. God wants to use you to reach His children. He stands by, ready to equip those servants who would dare to pray and ask for assistance.

Concluding Thoughts on Prayer

"Those who care about children will make a deeper commitment and provide long-term relationships and endless love that make faith community God's unique context for His kind of ministry with boys and girls."[20]

Paul said it best in 1 Thessalonians 2:8: "We loved you so much, we were delighted to share with you not only the gos-

---

19 Spurgeon, *Come Ye Children*, 157.
20 Richards, *A Theology*, 376.

pel of God but our lives as well." We must move beyond the "professionalism" of children's evangelism. It is time to commit ourselves all-out to introducing children to Christ. It is time to share our lives as well.

Spurgeon wrote, "Remember who it is that works by your feeble instrumentality."[21] We must remember that it is God who works in and through us to draw in the children. He wants them to be saved and come to the knowledge of the truth.

This chapter has taken one small slice of a huge pie and given you a taste. I've written about prayer and the children's leader. You've read about the personal prayer life of the children's leader. After this, I took a look at the importance of prayer in child evangelism.

Ed Silvoso wrote, "What is the Spirit saying to the churches? My observation is that the Spirit is delivering a dual emphasis—prayer and evangelism. And He is doing it in such a way that it reads like one message delivered in stereo."[22] God is still sending the same message. And it is still dual in its emphasis—prayer and evangelism. This prayer and evangelism cry includes the gospel presentation to, and conversion of, His little ones.

The children's leader must not close his ears to the heart cry of God in this matter. The evangelism of boys and girls is close to the heart of God. "Children need the gospel, the whole gospel, the unadulterated gospel; they ought to have it, and if they are taught of the Spirit of God they are as capable of receiving it as persons of ripe years."[23]

---

21 Spurgeon, *Come Ye Children*, 150.

22 Silvoso, *That None Should Perish*, 13.

23 Spurgeon, *Come Ye Children*, 74.

With God's help and a renewed commitment to prayer, child evangelism will move ahead with power. In my own life and ministry, I will pray more so I can do more so I can help more children until Jesus returns. I encourage you to take time right now and evaluate your approach to children's evangelism through a filter of prayer. Work to increase the prayer emphasis in your personal, family, and corporate life. Strive to make prayer a large part of any evangelistic opportunity in which God allows you to take part.

CHAPTER 8
PROMOTING YOUR MINISTRY

"Let someone else praise you, and not your own mouth;
an outsider, and not your own lips." —Proverbs 27:2

Promoting your ministry is a necessary part of serving as a children's leader. Some may think it wrong or "unspiritual" to promote yourself to others, but survival of children's ministry in the local church is dependent on a solid approach to promotion.

Promotional strategy should be simple yet well planned. Implementation of this strategy is foundational for those wishing to recruit more workers, gain more budgetary dollars, and achieve more visibility. Promotion in the local church should be approached on three levels—targeting the pastor, the people, and the public.

The Pastor

Your senior pastor is God's authority in the local church. As such, don't you think he is entitled to know all he can about your ministry? I have always served under positive-thinking pastors. Get in the habit of testifying to your pastor. Many children's workers will only approach the pastor when there are problems. Negative reports are the last thing a pastor wants to hear from you on a Sunday morning. Tell him about one great thing that happened in your ministry that morning. Eventually he will learn that the children's ministry at his church is a vibrant, growing, positive experience. He may even begin to repeat your testimonies from the pulpit.

Do your homework. When approaching the pastor concerning annual budget proposals or projects that you wish to launch, be ready. Scripture says, "Do your best to present yourself to God as one approved, a worker who does not need to be ashamed . . ." (2 Timothy 2:15). I say, do your best to present yourself to God and to your senior pastor. Lay out specifics in your budget or project work. Attempt to answer all the questions that your pastor may ask. Do this in a neat, logical order on paper. I have never been disappointed when approaching my pastor with a well-thought-out plan.

Drop notes of thanks and testimony to your pastor. Let him know what is happening in your life and ministry. Don't wait for the annual pastor appreciation day to thank your pastor. It is an honor to serve in the ministry. You are serving with a forward-thinking pastor who had enough wisdom to know his church needed a children's pastor. Thank him regularly with honest, heartfelt thanks.

Remember, a little schmooze goes a long way. Do what you can to promote the pastor's vision and ministry. Love on him and his vision and you will receive a return. You are the key promoter of the children and ministry to him in your church. Do all you can to present to your pastor a positive image of this ministry. Involve the children and workers in praying for the pastor. Then let him know you are doing this. With the advent of digital photo technology, you can snap a few pictures each week and e-mail copies to the pastor.

All these are ways to promote your ministry to the pastor. In none of these have I encouraged you to praise your personal involvement or exaggerate results. Keep an honest scorecard, and your pastor will recognize your integrity. Check your attitude and make certain that you are a grateful servant loving the children, families, leaders, and, above all, your pastor.

The People

The life of your children's ministry is largely dependent on lay involvement. People's perception of your ministry will draw them in or drive them away. How many times have you heard horror stories about the worker who was coerced into service with three-year-olds? Five years later this burned-out teacher is still serving and is wondering why the children's pastor hasn't stopped for a visit.

The people of your church are your finest resource. Your children's ministry will succeed if the people are behind it. When I began my work as a children's pastor, I assumed that most of my time would be spent with children. I quickly discovered that the majority of my time was spent ministering to and working side by side with the parents and adults who served the children.

Do all you can to love the people of your church. Remember the law of sowing and reaping. "Do not be deceived: God cannot be mocked. A man reaps what he sows" (Galatians 6:7). Plant your life and your love into the people and you will reap a harvest of life and love in return. Here are some things to remember in promoting your ministry to the people.

Be Genuine

Adults don't always see a phony right away, but kids will know it in a flash. Be yourself. If you don't like yourself, work on who you are. Do all you can to become a personable, likable, joy-filled believer. Your genuine joy, love, and concern for people cannot be hidden.

Be Alert

Scripture says, "watch and pray" (Matthew 26:41). There have been times when I was so intent on accomplishing my "job" that I failed to notice the needs of those around me. Watch and listen to people. When I began my ministry in Bloomington, Minnesota, my Sunday school coordinator, Marcella, had a simple need: she had been requesting new card tables for registration for several months. Apparently no one had heard her cries. I went down to Walmart and purchased those tables the first week. Marcella was happy and served faithfully the eight years I worked at that church.

Be Prayerful

Pray for the people. Pray for boys and girls and teens and moms and dads. Pray for grandparents. When a child or adult brings a prayer request to you, pray immediately. Let the people know that your ministry is built on the solid foundation of prayer. Invite workers and children to join you in prayer often. Host all-church prayer meetings for the children. Assign children's names to your senior citizens so that they may pray for the boys and girls daily.

The Public

I have been blessed to work alongside some very creative men and women in this area of promotion. Pastor Keith Kerstetter, together with Merlin Quiggle, invented some wonderful promotional campaigns for my ministry and the other ministries of our church. These men designed and ran advertisements in our local newspapers. They set up a rotational schedule to promote all church ministries in our own bulletin and in the community.

Pastor Keith walked into my office one day and showed me a newspaper ad which featured a large photo of a preschool child holding a stuffed dinosaur in her arms. The ad encouraged parents to look beyond the training their children could receive from a purple dinosaur. It went on to suggest that they and their children might do well to visit our church.

Organize quarterly events that will appeal to the un-churched of your community. Make these big and exciting and child-friendly. My friend Brian is children's pastor on Maui. He hosts a community-wide Easter egg hunt each year. This is one of the biggest events on his island. Hundreds of children and adults come out for the fun and the gospel message.

Utilize every avenue available in promoting your ministry to the community. Newspapers, radio, flyers, and cable TV can be used in promotion. Do what you can to cooperate with local schools, libraries, and public service agencies. Cooperate with law enforcement and your community park and recreations depart-ment. My church hosted a "We Love Kids Banquet" each Febru-ary. This was done in cooperation with our community campaign entitled, "Bloomington Loves Its Kids Month" (Bloomington, Minnesota, Parks and Recreation Department).

Remember, a great ministry can fail for lack of promotion. If you have something worth participating in, then it is worth promoting. Do all you can to build bridges of promotion with your pastor, your people, and your public.

DEVELOPING EVANGELISTIC EVENTS

Many churches, regardless of size, host one or two evangelistic events for children each year. These events can be as simple as a special emphasis one Sunday at Christmastime or as elaborate as a five-day vacation Bible school. I recommend that you start small. If your church is not used to running big events, then keep it simple. Plan a special emphasis Sunday once or twice a year. Use these to develop systems for running larger events. I'll go into the specifics of how to do this in a few paragraphs.

When planning an event, you must first determine your purpose. The purpose of the event will inform your planning and presentation of Christ and the gospel. Will the event be introductory, Christian training, or evangelistic?

Introductory Events

I've mentioned earlier in this work that a presentation of the gospel, with opportunity for children to respond, should be made in every club, class, or service. I stray from that on occasion when an event's purpose is one of introduction to the church, Christianity, and your ministry. Some churches host events to feed the poor, provide care or training for parents and children of divorce, or simply enjoy a party. I have been part of two churches that each ran an open house night. This was a night when families could tour our facility, meet teachers and other leaders, enjoy snacks, and have fun. If your event is introductory, you may want to back off from the hard-sell altar time and allow the presentation of the gospel to be more organic. In these kinds of events, leaders will answer questions, share God's love in a variety of ways, and provide take-home materials explaining salvation. A gift bag can be prepared for each child or family attending your introductory event.

Christian Training Events

The theme of these events will be to instruct or further disciple children and families who have already made a commitment to Christ. Some vacation Bible school curriculums lend themselves to being training events. Keep in mind that although the expectation is that children have already made a first-time commitment to Christ, there may be unchurched and even unsaved children in attendance. Keep your language child-friendly throughout the event. Never presuppose biblical knowledge. In a training event there will be children who have known Jesus since they were toddlers grouped with those who have just been introduced to Christ. Be ready to explain everything. Once again, prepare gift bags or other take-home materials that provide reinforcement for your teaching and a clear presentation of the gospel.

Evangelistic Events

I participate in a church that hosts a breakfast Sunday each quarter. On this Sunday, we set up pancake and waffle stations and serve fruit, coffee, juices, and pastries. Families enjoy breakfast together, and then an abbreviated version of our morning service is held. The gospel is presented on a practical, nonthreatening level to people of all ages. My son Aaron was children's pastor at a church that held an annual VBS. Everything was designed to present Christ in a loving way to the children and their parents. Children learned songs and memorized Bible verses to be presented in a family night at the end of the best week of their summer.

Be sure that your evangelistic event is fun, safe, family-friendly, and will attract children in your community. Create easy-to-use promotional materials such as postcards or invitations that are colorful and creative. These can be distributed to the children and their parents with simple instruction on how to invite their neighbors to participate in the event.

Once you have determined the purpose of your big event, establish a date and time. But allow me to back up just a bit. Remember that I told you I would help you understand how to run your event, whether large or small? Of course you do. The first thing to do when planning an event is to gather some trusted leaders in your church and form an event committee. A VBS or breakfast Sunday requires organization. Your committee or event planning team may only need to work for a couple of weeks for a smaller event. But for larger events they may work together for as long as ten months in advance. Meet with your team as often as needed, depending on the complexity of your event. I like to start meeting once or twice a month and then meet each week as the event draws nearer.

Your committee needs to be in on the planning as early as possible. Allowing them the luxury of establishing the purpose, theme, date, and length of an event gives them ownership. I know it's easier for you to do this on your own. But when your team owns the event, each member becomes a cheerleader for the success of what you want to accomplish. Each member begins to share their vision and enthusiasm with others in the church. Before long, you have extra helpers wanting to take part.

Once a committee establishes the purpose, theme, and date, a timeline must be established. Call it a countdown. This countdown lists everything that needs to be done, and the order in which to do it, between now and your big event. Team members then step forward to lead each important aspect of this plan. One will take care of promotions, another decorations, and another the program to be presented. Divide the tasks in such a way that everyone feels needed and can shine, using their gifts to contribute to the success of the whole.

Let me share a few words about the theme. The theme for your event should be understandable. Can the youngest child in the room understand your theme? Can it be easily explained to somebody with no biblical knowledge? Is it possibly offensive to a sector of society? Is it easy to repeat and remember? I have looked over the years at the incredible variety of vacation Bible school themes that come out each summer. The publishers have already done the hard work of answering the questions above. Remember that your church will be hearing about this theme for several months in some cases. You do not want people to tire of it before the event.

I once planned an outreach week for our church. This was something that we did for several summers. I called it "Neighborhood Outreach Week." I wrote the service material and then trained clowns, puppeteers, storytellers, and song leaders. Our teams went out to three different neighborhoods each morning that week. One of my team members mentioned in passing that she thought more people would come if we changed the name to

"Side-Yard Party." I listened. So instead of signs posted saying, "Neighborhood Outreach Week," we had signs made saying, "Come to a Side-Yard Party." Our outreach doubled because of her suggestion.

A big event may be held one day, several days, or even for a week. It could involve food, entertainment, and an actual service. Whatever the purpose or makeup of the event, following up with your attendees is important. You will want to invite children and families to return for other Sundays and events at your church. So, how do you gather information to follow up with those attending?

The simple, traditional way to do this is to register each person who attends. Churches have developed all kinds of systems for this. You may simply provide a registration card to be filled out as children enter the building that day. Some churches have generated a registration page on a website dedicated to the event. Children can pre-register through the site days or weeks in advance. I've seen tablets set up in the church lobby. Children sign up and sign in each time they attend the four-night event. Names that are gathered will be used in follow-up endeavors.

Incentives are sometimes offered to encourage children to sign in to the event. Door prizes, random prize giveaways, or special items to be sent to each home after the event are some examples of these.

Follow-up includes ongoing connection with children and their families. Invitations are sent for future events and special activities. Some churches send out discipleship materials or provide downloadable coloring pages for children and families. Above all, let the people know that you care about them and love them. A kind, loving invitation or informational help for a single parent can go a long way toward establishing goodwill with a new family.

I've talked for a few pages about developing evangelistic events. Perhaps you've never run an event for the children. Try it. Begin small and see what happens. Special Sundays and other events not only excite the children of your church, but they become a conduit to the children of your community. Perhaps boys and girls will come to Christ during your fall festival this year. Or maybe they will become excited to share the gospel with other children through your Saturday missions retreat. Whatever the event, I know that you can provide joy and the opportunity to experience new life in Christ through events at your church.

CHAPTER 10

LEADING A CHILD TO CHRIST

In order to prepare yourself to reach children in group outreach settings, you must first examine appropriate methods in leading an individual child to Christ. This chapter will begin in the Bible and then explore some dos and don'ts of leading a child to Christ.

The following Scriptures are all verses commonly used to lead adults to Christ: Romans 3:23; 6:23; John 1:11–12; 1 John 1:9; and Acts 16:31. Take note that these and other "salvation" verses provide no age-level boundaries. Every person, young or old, can obtain the promise of salvation according to Scripture. Children are not discarded by the biblical text. In fact, Jesus emphasized our bringing them to Him in Matthew 19:14. And, after telling the story of the lost sheep in Matthew 18:10–13, Jesus says, "In the same way your Father in heaven is not willing that any of these little ones should perish" (Matthew 18:14). He is emphasizing the importance of the salvation of children in the eyes of our heavenly Father.

Before leading a child to Christ, the church leader must ask, "Why?" The answers are simple. First, and most important, the act of leading a child to Christ is a fulfillment of the Great Commission. We are to win and disciple every person, young or old. The act of winning a child is an act of loving rescue. We are rescuing the perishing. If you believe a child can spend eternity without Christ, then you must be compelled to rescue that child for Christ.

Second, children are the easiest age group to reach with the gospel. I remind you that George Barna discovered this in his research.[1] The act of winning a child takes less effort, producing a greater return on investment, than winning an adult or teenager. A child won to Christ at an early age can grow in fruitful Christian service all of her life. The adult coming to Christ has oftentimes already squandered half a lifetime in sinful living.

Finally, leading a child to Christ is an act of faith. By faith, you are winning and discipling a future generation of Christian leadership. A child certainly can lead within the scope of his or her gifts while young. The wise worker leads a child to Christ and then through intentional discipleship cultivates that child's gifts for leadership in tomorrow's church. By faith, the child becomes the face of future Christianity on planet Earth.

Now that you know why a child should be won, what are some basics you should know about leading them to Christ?

Be kind and loving. Your gentle spirit will do much to encourage the child that Christ is a loving and kind Savior. It is a testimony to Christ's saving power when a kind and loving adult confronts a child for Christ. Many adults in a child's life only address the child in a cold, commanding tone. Even that is done in the context of social imprinting. Adults train children in table manners, basic safety, and appropriate interaction with others. It is rare that Christ becomes the center of discussion.

---

1   George Barna, *Transforming Children into Spiritual Champions* (Ventura: Regal Books, 2003), 34. "We discovered that the probability of someone embracing Jesus as his or her Savior was 32% for those between the ages of 5 and 12; 4% for those in the 13 to 18 age range; and 6% for people 19 or older."

Your presentation of Christ using loving words and a kind spirit will do much to convince the child of his need for the Savior.

Use kid language. Christianity and its benefits must be explained in a manner understood by the prospective convert. Whether winning a tribal chief in Kenya or a little girl in Waukee, Iowa, the evangelist must use language and concepts understood by the listener. The culture of childhood can rarely comprehend the language and examples provided by many adult preachers. Speak in kid-friendly terminology.

Avoid abstract concepts. Children grow from concrete thinking to abstract thinking sometime in their mid- to late-elementary years. Phrases like, "Let Jesus wash you in His blood" or "Ask Him to come into your heart" should be avoided. I once met a boy who was convinced his grandfather died because Jesus was in his heart. He explained that Jesus couldn't fit so his "grandfather's heart got broken."

Speak softly. Loud volume and aggressive tone of voice can often scare a child. Soften your approach to things of God. Let the child come to Jesus. This is not a time to be argumentative or pushy. Relax your voice and attitude.

Make no presupposition of biblical knowledge. Your genuine love and respect for a child will compel you to explain any biblical reference fully. The unchurched and unsaved child may have no idea who Jesus, David the shepherd boy, or Jonah is. When dropping a reference to any Bible story or verse, explain it in plain, understandable language. Approach every salvation encounter as if it is the first time the child has heard the good news.

Ask questions. Allow the child to discover God's truth. Open a Bible. If old enough, encourage the child to read a highlighted verse. After reading it, ask what the verse means to him. Let the child answer in his own way and with his own words. Do not rush this process.

Allow the child to ask questions. Nothing is off-limits when a soul is in need of the Savior. Through the interaction of asking and answering questions, the child can come to terms with her need for Jesus. When you think you have explained the message adequately, ask the child what she wants to do. Is she ready to give her life to Jesus? Is he ready to put his faith and trust in Jesus to forgive his sin and become his Savior?

Once the message has been explained, and understood fully, it's *time to pray*. Some employ a call-and-response style prayer. You know the kind. It goes something like this: Dear Jesus . . . DEAR JESUS . . . I know you love me. . . . I KNOW YOU LOVE ME. . . . and so on.[2] Remember that prayer should never be forced. If the child is not ready to give his life to Christ, simply close in a prayer that reminds the child of what was discussed. If he is ready, pray the child through to Jesus. I will always encourage a child to pray in his own words after concluding a call-and-response prayer.

Remember the word S.I.N.G. when praying. Speak conversationally, Involve the child, No churchy adult-speak, and Give God the glory. By the way, God wants the child to join His family more than you do. Let the Holy Spirit put the pressure on as you relax and reap a harvest.

There are some practices that should be left behind. The first of these is assuming the child wants to be saved when he has not expressed that need. Children will respond at altars in

---

2   The prayer I often use in call-and-response is as follows: "Dear Jesus. I just heard that you love me. You died on the cross for me. I believe you rose from the dead. I want to live for you. I have sinned. I've done wrong. I have disobeyed your Word, the Bible. I've hurt others with actions, with words, and with my attitudes. I AM SORRY. Please forgive me. I have sinned. Wash my sin away. Make me clean and new. I trust you to save me. Be my Savior. Be my friend. Amen."

whatever way the leader calls for response. The child may be concerned about his grandmother, worried about school, or just feeling God's presence. The leader tells children to come to the front of the room and then assumes all children present wish to be saved. Inquire why a boy has come down front to pray. You might ask, "What do you want God to do today?" You may find he needs prayer for something other than the salvation message just presented. Pray for that urgently felt need. Then, if he is open, approach his relationship with the Savior.

Do not insist upon or force a conversion/commitment. Let children come to Jesus. Your enthusiasm or pushiness may compel a child to pray, but there will be no genuine conversion. I say again, relax. Let God do the work of salvation in a child's life. When he or she is ready, then pray.

Some present God as a cruel judge. This kind of presentation will scare children into praying even if they are not ready. Stay away from stories of God's harsh judgment on people or nations. It was a common practice in the 1970s for evangelists to tell scary stories of people and animals giving their lives to spare others. At the conclusion of such stories, children would be invited to pray. Many children prayed out of empathy for the poor dead chicken or family member in the story. There is no place for scaring children into making a commitment to Christ.

Never work one-on-one behind closed doors with a child wanting to be saved. Always follow the three-person rule. This rule demands that there be three or more people present in every church ministry setting. The wise children's leader always has another worker by her side when praying with children. The altar area in most churches is out in the open and a safe place to pray. If moving to a quieter part of the room, invite another child or worker to join you.

Here are some things to do when leading a child to Christ. First, celebrate salvation. Your joy and excitement when a child responds to Christ should be evident. This is a happy occasion. The child has accepted Jesus. Celebrate the win.

Be sure that throughout the entire process you listen to the child. You may have to step back and slow down in your presentation. You may need to explain something you thought was a given. By listening to the child, you can adjust your comments and cater to her needs.

Use mouthwash and deodorant. I know, you didn't want me to go there, but a stinky worker can distract a child. Take care of your breath and hygiene. You would never want that to deter a child from accepting Christ because of bad breath.

Ask God for wisdom. Seek the Holy Spirit's guidance. The salvation of any person is accomplished by a work of the Holy Spirit. You and I cannot save anybody. We can only introduce the child to Christ and encourage prayer. The Holy Spirit does the heart-changing work of salvation.

Now let me share a word about parents in this process. Whenever possible, include parents when leading and praying with their child. There is no greater joy I've experienced as a dad, grandpa, and children's leader than praying with one of my children to accept Christ. If the parents are handy, include them in the discussion and subsequent prayer. If they are not, contact and talk with them as soon as possible. This should be done personally, not via social media. Parents don't want to read about it when they can hear from you and ask questions. Celebrate the child's decision with mom and/or dad.

Be sure to follow up with every child who comes to Christ. Develop your own materials or utilize some of the fine discipleship products found online. Write or call children regularly to check up on their growth in Christ. Include the parents and other children in this ongoing follow-up endeavor.

We've explored biblical and practical aspects of leading a child to Christ. I purposely left out a script to follow. The presentation of a plan of salvation should be as natural to a Christian as receiving Communion. Prepare ahead of time by making note of or highlighting Bible verses you would like to use. Pray that God will assist you in becoming fruitful in this effort. Remember always to be patient, let God be God, and continue to share God's great plan of salvation every chance you get. May God bless you as you lead children into a relationship with Him.

CHAPTER 11

LEADING CHILDREN INTO THE BAPTISM IN THE HOLY SPIRIT

(This first appeared in *Helping Others Receive the Gift*, edited by Tim Enloe)

For over thirty years, I have been involved in children's church, crusades, and children's camps. I have witnessed to, led, and prayed for hundreds of children to receive the Baptism in the Holy Spirit. I have seen this gift distributed freely among boys and girls as young as four and five years old. I have stood by as children praying for other children spoke words of wisdom, helping their friends understand and receive this unique gift. In this chapter, I will share with you some practical insights on leading children into the Baptism in the Holy Spirit.

I interviewed over a hundred children a few years back while speaking at a statewide children's camp. Not one of them could tell me about the Baptism in the Holy Spirit. Only two had ever heard of speaking with other tongues. It was as if I had been transported to Acts chapter 19 and was standing alongside of Paul as the Ephesian believers told him, "We have not even heard that there is a Holy Spirit."[1] By Thursday night of that week,

---

1   Acts 19:1–6.

most of those children could not only explain what the Baptism in the Holy Spirit was, they had experienced this wonderful gift.

So how did that happen? What approach did I take at those altars? When do you know it is the right time to pray? Let's look at these and other questions so that we can better understand how to lead children in this important aspect of Christian living.

Let the Children Learn

We want our children to experience the best quality teaching when it comes to the basics of reading, writing, and arithmetic. We do what we can to ensure that our school systems provide well-trained, pleasant teachers who make learning a joy for the young ones. Then the kids come to church. Do they deserve less than the best on Sunday mornings? Children must have competent people of good character training them in biblical truths. Children need solid, interesting teaching when it comes to spiritual matters. In no other spiritual aspect is this more important than the Baptism in the Holy Spirit.

So how do you, as the children's teacher or leader, approach this subject? First look to the Bible. What does it say about this gift and about children receiving it? In Acts 1:5 Jesus says, "For John baptized with water, but in a few days you will be baptized with the Holy Spirit." It is important for children to know that Jesus used the term *baptized* when referring to this second gift. We are talking about a promise of God.

In Luke 11, when teaching on prayer, Jesus uses an illustration that any child can understand: "Which of you fathers, if your son asks for a fish, will give him a snake instead? Or if he asks for an egg, will give him a scorpion? If you then, though you are evil, know how to give good gifts to your children, how much more will your Father in heaven give the Holy Spirit to those who ask him!" (Luke 11:11-13). I have used this simple illustration many times in assuring children that when they ask God sincerely for this gift, He will not allow them to fake it or receive a counterfeit. I also use this passage to encourage children to ask God for this gift.

I usually include Acts 2:39 when talking with children about this gift. It reads, "The promise is for you and your children and for all who are far off—for all whom the Lord our God will call." Even if you choose to generalize the word *children* in this passage, you cannot ignore the context that would include all believers, young and old, throughout history.

It is important when teaching children to incorporate all of the senses. While speaking the Word will have some impact, causing it to come alive using everyday objects will have a lasting impact. Over the years I have developed several teachings using everyday objects when approaching the Baptism in the Holy Spirit with children. Here are two that work well.

The Bike: Place an ordinary child's bicycle in front of the children. Turn it upside down, standing it on the handlebars and seat. Invite a child to come to the front of the room and assist you. Place a bike helmet on that child and talk about the helmet of salvation. Just as a bike rider must wear a helmet as he rides, the child must be saved before seeking the Baptism in the Holy Spirit. This is a gift reserved for those who believe. The Ephesians of Acts 19 listened to Paul, accepted the Word, were baptized in water showing their newfound commitment to Christ, and *then* hands were laid on them to receive the Holy Spirit.

My child assistant is then instructed to point to the front tire while turning the pedals and thus empowering the rear tire. I talk about the Baptism in the Holy Spirit being like a bike. A bicycle comes with two tires, front and rear. The front tire gives the ride balance and direction. This is what a prayer language does. The back tire gives power to move forward. Again, this is what the power of the Holy Spirit does for the believer.

Nobody would think of trying to ride a bike that was missing a tire. The bike has a front and rear tire, while the Baptism in the Holy Spirit provides the believer with power and a prayer language. Every time a child rides a bike or sees someone riding, he can remember the blessing of the Baptism in the Holy Spirit.

Receiving is as easy as riding a bike. At first you may use training wheels or receive encouragement from a parent or older sibling. When receiving the Holy Spirit you may use the training wheels of verbal praise while receiving encouragement from a friend or pastor as you praise God.

Once you have received power and a prayer language as the Spirit baptizes you, be sure to use that gift every day. Nobody would buy a brand-new bike and park it in the garage all year. A child with a bike will ride it every chance he gets. He would not save it to ride one week a summer or on special days only. A bike gives a boy or girl freedom. The Baptism will do the same, giving a child freedom to grow into a deeper walk with God.

The Kid's Meal: Purchase any kid's meal from a local fast-food franchise. I bring five children up front and allow each to hold a different part of the kid's meal. I take a little time to talk about each part and compare it to an aspect of the Baptism in the Holy Spirit. I then remind all of the children to remember these things when they eat a kid's meal. This lesson will include the following components:

- Bag or box = The Bible, which holds all we know about the Holy Spirit
- Prize = Speaking in tongues—most people go for this prize first

- Meat = Power of the Holy Spirit—received when Baptized in the Holy Spirit
- Fries = Extra gifts like prophecy or tongues and interpretation
- Fountain drink = The joy of the Lord

Be certain to explain fully what will happen when you pray with the children for this gift. I have found many children to be afraid of the unknown. They do not break through in prayer because of a hidden fear. Sometime in the presentation of this gift I will address fears that children may have. Some of those expressed to me by children include uncontrollable tongue talking, blacking out, being shaken by adult workers, or prophetic information coming into their brain like an explosion. One girl mentioned that she was afraid of praying because she might get slain in the Spirit and hit her head on the floor. I encouraged her to go ahead and just lie down. That way if God did slay her in the Spirit she would not hit her head, as she would already be on the floor. She lay down, and after a few moments of prayer was baptized in the Holy Spirit with no physical injury.

Let the Children Come

"Jesus said, 'Let the little children come to me, and do not hinder them, for the kingdom of heaven belongs to such as these'" (Matthew 19:14). Letting children come to Jesus implies a kind invitation. For too many years, well-meaning Pentecostals have implored, pressured, scared, or even coerced children to come to altars to pray for the Baptism in the Holy Spirit. It was almost as if the receiving of the gift took importance over the practical application of the gift. Where is the fruit of the

Spirit in an altar service that would press children to receive a gift for which they are not ready?

Children's leader, I implore you to LET the children come! Do not drag, threaten, trick, push, or pull children towards Jesus and the gifts He has for them. Do not tell scary stories that force them into a place of uncomfortable decision.

Mike introduced himself to me during the first altar service at a camp in Humble, Texas. As other children were praying, he approached me and said, "I don't want to pray." Rather than try to force the goodness of God on this eleven-year-old boy, I replied, "Then just sit back and watch, Mike. If you have any questions, just find me and ask." The second and third nights of camp, a similar exchange took place. Then came Thursday night's service. Mike came up to me with tears running down his face and blurted out, "I'm ready now." Mike accepted Jesus as his Savior and was baptized in the Spirit at that altar. I am sure that had I forced the issue earlier in the week, he would not have received.

I have found over the years that children want more of God. Scripture says, "Taste and see that the Lord is good" (Psalm 34:8). Our task as leaders is to present Jesus in such a way that children will want to taste and see. Once they have had a taste of genuine prayer and praise, they will develop a hunger that will last a lifetime. The Baptism in the Holy Spirit is a wonderful gift that, once received, will give children the kind of hunger I am talking about.

My wife, Darlene, and I have four children. There have been times in each one of their lives that we have sat waiting at the dinner table as they tried a new food. Forcing this upon them rarely resulted in their wanting more of the mystery substance. We learned that presentation of a new food alongside of other dishes they loved was a much better approach. In the same way, presenting a gift like the Baptism in the Holy Spirit can be done in such a way as to excite the child's imagination and engage the child's desire for more of God. Forcing a child to "taste and see" this experience will reap little benefit in his or her life.

You will want to present the Baptism in the Holy Spirit and all that comes with it in a positive light. Illustrate the message in such a way as to water the garden of enthusiasm in their hearts. I've given you a couple of ideas for illustration, but so many more exist. It is important when presenting this lesson to illustrate it in a colorful, simple, child-friendly manner. Use objects, stories, and music that appeal to the child's senses and sensibility. Involve the children in the lesson. Do not hold an object yourself when you can employ a child in holding it for you. Do not just tell a story, but bring children up front to act it out.

It is important that you do not use scare tactics or spooky stories. Face it, some of the spiritual happenings surrounding adults receiving this gift can sound scary when explained to a child. The idea of suddenly speaking in an unknown tongue can be frightening to a child. Here is how I explain tongues:

"God will do nothing scary to you. He does not come in and move your tongue uncontrollably. That would be scary. You praise Him in your native tongue and He will give you new words through your mind and spirit. You may hear or think a word or two. Say those words by faith as God gives you more and more of His Spirit. The words you say or language God gives you may not sound anything like me or others speaking around you. That's okay. God loves you so much that He wants to give you a special unique prayer language that you can use when you don't know how to pray."

It is important to note that we want to encourage children to seek more of God. Certainly at Christmastime you want to receive gifts from your grandparents. But the experience is so much richer when you get to do that with grandpa or grandma in the room to hug and love you. I encourage children not to worry about getting tongues, but instead to enjoy spending time with Jesus. Scripture says, "I love those who love me, and those who seek me find me" (Proverbs 8:17). In another place it says, "Come near to God and he will come near to you" (James 4:8).

Jesus didn't say, "Wait in Jerusalem until you speak in tongues." Speaking in other tongues is the initial physical evidence of having received the Baptism in the Holy Spirit. The tongues will happen when a child receives. But emphasis must be placed not on "getting tongues," but on being empowered by Jesus. Boys and girls need the power of the Holy Spirit in order to stand for Him in these last days. To seek the gift without the Giver is to make the same mistake Simon did in Acts 8:18.

Let the Children Pray

Children are full of faith and ready to pray at any time. In both camp and church settings I have discovered that if we allow children to pray and give them time to do this, they will respond by storming the gates of heaven. One Sunday morning I opened the altars to children wishing to receive the Baptism in the Holy Spirit. About a dozen children responded. When I invited friends to pray with these children, more than thirty came down to help their peers. The prayer service went on so long that parents were coming in the back of the room. We invited these parents to join their children in prayer. Many did, and God moved in a marvelous way.

Stanley Grenz writes, "Many Christians do not pray because they are not convinced that prayer works; they do not understand what prayer is, how prayer functions, or for what they should pray."[2] If this is true of the adult believers about whom Stanley Grenz writes, how much more is it true of children. So our task as leaders of children is to help boys and girls experience God in real ways. We must teach on prayer, but not stop until children have experienced what we have taught about.

Children approach God with simple, genuine faith. How many times has a child approached you asking that you pray for a plant, pet, or parent? The child who asks does not hesitate to believe that you will pray and God will hear you. This same basic faith is utilized when a child prays to receive spiritual gifts from God. Once a child is allowed to come to Him, that child will receive from Him.

Don Crawford writes, "We call not on a father who is preoccupied with his career and has little time for his children. We call not on a father who may find someone else he loves more and so forsake us. Nor does the father on whom we call simply cater to our whims while we manipulate him."[3] God is always available to listen to and answer the prayers of children.

I had a group of Royal Rangers commanders who wanted to host a Holy Spirit night in their third-grade group. They laid out the plan for the evening and invited me to come pray for children at about 7:30 that evening. They taught and readied the boys, and in my absence began to pray. I arrived in the room at about 7:45 to the sound of two dozen third-grade boys on their faces before God, praying their hardest. Several boys had received the Holy Spirit prior to my entering the room. These boys were praying for and encouraging friends to receive this gift.

---

2   Stanley Grenz, *Prayer: A Cry for The Kingdom* (Peabody, MA: Hendrickson Publishers, 1988), 47.

3   Dan Crawford, *The Prayer-Shaped Disciple* (Peabody, MA: Hendrickson Publishers, 1999), 5.

Boys and girls will pray if we will allow it. They will wait before God if we give them time to do so. They will receive the good gifts of God if we encourage them.

Let the Children Enjoy God

Finally, I would like to address the concept of letting children enjoy the presence of God. Seeking the Baptism in the Holy Spirit should not be painful, distressing, or scary for any child. Yet I have talked with children and adults who sought this gift as a child who have had tragic experiences at altars.

One man told me that every leader who came through his church shook him and yelled at him and tried to somehow force the gift into him. This man didn't receive the Holy Spirit until he was in his late twenties. This brings to mind the fact that you, as a leader of children, are not the baptizer. Let God be God and baptize children when they are ready and when the time is right. There is nothing you can do to force this experience to happen. You cannot yell loud enough or say the magic formula to cause this to happen in children's lives. Let Jesus gently draw children in.

I have met many children who, when leaving the altar without having received, felt guilty or insignificant. One girl cried that if she didn't go home from camp with the gift of tongues, her mom would be upset. Whatever happened to trusting God? How can we as leaders feel justified in presenting a wonderful gift like the Baptism in the Holy Spirit in such a way that those who do not receive it feel like second-class believers?

I exhort you to encourage every child who prays for this gift. I talk to children at the conclusion of or following an altar service. I congratulate all who have prayed. I encourage those who have received to use that prayer language every chance they get. I encourage those who have not yet received to walk believing. They have asked God to fill them to overflowing with His Spirit. He is going to do this in their lives. I tell them, "Walk away from this altar expecting that any minute now the overflowing will happen and you will speak in another tongue."

One group of about a dozen ten- and eleven-year-old girls came excitedly jabbering to me after an altar service in a hotel meeting room. By their own testimony, all had prayed for most of an hour. None had received. They chose to go back to their rooms believing that God would baptize them at any minute. When they all entered the elevator with their counselor, one girl hit the button for their floor. When her finger touched that button, everyone on that elevator was baptized in the Spirit.

A nine-year-old boy shared with me at breakfast one day that he was walking to the restroom in the middle of the night. As he walked, he was singing a worship song. Soon the words he was singing were not English.

One group of girls in Missouri decided to hold hands and pray before starting a volleyball game one afternoon at camp. As they prayed for the soon-to-start game, the Holy Spirit came upon them. Both teams were simultaneously baptized in the Spirit right there by the volleyball net. They had so much fun praying that they didn't get around to playing.

I could go on and on with more such testimonies. I think you get my point. When we, as leaders of children, make this experience a Jesus thing, kids will receive and will have a great time doing so. Relax and let God do His thing. In camp and crusade settings there is a certain amount of pressure placed on leaders and preachers to produce results. Set that pressure aside in favor of allowing children to enjoy being in the presence of God.

One night at camp in Minnesota, Jon, then ten years old, was gloriously filled with the Spirit. He sang and prayed in his prayer language. He danced and jumped and ran through the altar service for over a half an hour. All of that time Jon's eyes were closed and tears of joy were running off of his cheeks. I know some leaders who would have stopped him. I'm glad we didn't. Jon had a unique experience that I have never witnessed before or since that night.

Part of assisting children in enjoying this experience is instructing them concerning all of the extra manifestations that can occur when a person receives the gift of God. A child may cry one time, then pray and laugh another time. He or she may feel nothing while speaking in tongues or they may feel deep emotions. Boys and girls need to hear that this is normal.

Some have been "slain in the Spirit" while praying. Right next to them others are having just as valid a prayer experience without being slain. I have witnessed children give prophetic utterances, words of knowledge, and tongues and interpretation at altars. It is fun to be used of God! I encourage children to seek to be used and tell them that God will give them just the right gift at just the right time.

Conclusion

Here are some bullet points to remember that will help you to better serve the children when addressing the subject of the Baptism in the Holy Spirit.

- Stay away from extremes.
- Teach using simple terms.
- Encourage children to pray.
- Ask God for direction.

- Do not ignore this subject.
- You can be used of God.

Stay away from extremes

Extreme approaches to spiritual happenings can be really scary to younger children. Try not to overemphasize personal preferences over Scriptural imperatives. If the Bible isn't specific concerning method or manifestation, then seek God as to how He wants the service to progress.

Teach using simple terms

I am not proposing that you dumb down this gift or any presentation of it. Be a wise teacher and make certain that you are using child-friendly language and illustrations.

Encourage children to pray

I remind you that boys and girls love to pray. With a little encouragement, extending the time available, and a nice altar area, kids can and will pray until the parents drag them away. Prayer should be encouraged as an everyday Christian living habit.

Ask God for direction

Seek God whenever you plan to present this subject. I try not to hang my current presentation on success in the past. I seek God anew each time I present this and I ask for His anointing to be fresh.

Do not ignore this subject

You may be afraid of doing something wrong when presenting the Holy Spirit to children. Do not let that stop you from doing this. I believe that if you sincerely seek God's direction and have right motives in presenting this that God will come through for you. His desire is for boys and girls everywhere to receive all that He has for them. You can be God's instrument of blessing in the lives of the children you serve.

You can be used of God

When it comes to helping children to receive the Baptism in the Holy Spirit, God does not show favoritism. You may be uneducated or highly educated. You may be rich or poor. You may be a pastor or a parishioner. I implore you to set aside any inadequacies you may feel and trust God. He is the Baptizer, and He is extremely good at this. God has been blessing people for years. He will continue to do so. Let God bless the children through you as you present the Baptism in the Holy Spirit to His most-loved little ones.

APPENDIX A
WHY BRING THE GOSPEL TO CHILDREN

This is a chart constructed using materials from Lois Lebar's book, *Children in the Bible School*. It gives all her reasons for reaching children with the gospel.

Why Bring the Gospel to Children?

The Bible clearly teaches that Christ Jesus calls the children to himself.
The most favorable soil for sowing the seed of the Word is the plastic heart of the child.
Early childhood's natural faith and dependency are soon outgrown.
Habits of the first seven years are indelibly established.
Less time and effort are necessary to win many children to Christ than to win one adult.
Children open many homes for the gospel.
A teacher's own life is matured as he sees himself as God's child learning His higher ways.

Lebar, Lois E., *Children in the Bible School* (New Jersey: Fleming H. Revell Company, 1952), 19–30.

HALLO-WHAT?

Ideas for impacting your neighbors on October 31

by

© 2005 Dick Gruber

Hallo—What?

As Halloween approaches, parents often ask me, "Should we participate in Halloween?" Others ask, "How can we impact our neighbors on this night, this year?"

In answer to the first question, I say follow your convictions. The words of Jesus found in Matthew 5:14–16 can give some direction in this. It reads, "You are the light of the world. A town built on a hill cannot be hidden. Neither do people light a lamp and put it under a bowl. Instead they put it on its stand, and it gives light to everyone in the house. In the same way, let your light shine before men, that they may see your good deeds and glorify your Father in heaven."

The observance of Halloween has dubious beginnings at best. The celebration has progressed from its early superstitious roots to the costumed and candy-gathering event of today. Most children and families in our communities either do not know of its beginnings or choose to have fun in spite of past practices associated with this day.

Wearing a Costume?

Here are some guidelines to follow should your family and children choose to dress up this Halloween night.

- As a believer, you want to do "everything as unto the Lord." You also have a desire to honor and glorify your Savior in all that you do. In light of this, avoid scary, embarrassing, or disgusting costumes.
- Make certain that whatever the costume or makeup, you look your best for Jesus. Makeup should be neat, clean, and safe. Avoid the thrown-together or unkempt look.

- If you are walking the neighborhood, include light colors in your costume. In this way, those driving can easily see and avoid hitting you.

- I recommend that you and/or your children can dress in several categories of costumes. These include:
  - Bible person, place, or thing
  - Historical figure
  - Clown/animal

- Write and rehearse a short testimony that goes with your costume. That way when people acknowledge how cute or interesting you look, you can come back with a brief but poignant explanation that gives the listener something eternal to think about.

- Have fun. Christians should be the example of joy at any season. Jesus was the kind of guy you would invite to a party. The wedding at Cana is an example of this. So do what you can to show the joy of the Lord and the fun that a Christian can have.

- You may want to carry a gospel tract with your costume. This can be given to those who show interest when you explain who or what you are.

Further Thoughts

Churches have adapted to this night by hosting everything from "Trunk or Treat" in the church parking lot to "Light the Night" events in neighborhoods. Whether we throw a harvest party or not, children will be combing our neighborhoods asking for a handout on Halloween night. Kids will dress in costumes as cute or scary as their parents allow, while neighborhood homes will hand out everything from cheap penny candies to popcorn balls and peanut butter cups.

What is a Christian family to do? I've known some who turned out the lights and locked the doors. Again, I encourage you to act upon your convictions in this matter. If you choose to do nothing for children on Halloween, turn the light off on your porch so that passing children will not be disappointed when knocking on your unanswered door.

Halloween Outreach Guidelines

Here are a few simple guidelines for those who choose to bless children on Halloween.

Pray! Pray for your neighborhood and the children, parents, and strangers who will pass down your street. Pray for God's anointing on neighboring churches that are hosting outreach events on this night. Pray that God will make you and your home a lighthouse in this darkened world.

Ideas for those who are simply handing out candy:

- At the least hand out extra candy and a gospel tract. Christian bookstores carry some good ones geared just to children on this day.

- Smile, get happy, and hand out genuine compliments

with the candy and tract. You want your neighbors to know that yours is a household that loves children. A kind word concerning a costume or behavior will go a long way with the child and their accompanying parent.

- Don't be too in-your-face preachy. This is the only night all year on which children will come to your door asking for something good. Do not scare them off with obnoxious or offensive preaching delivered under the guise of witnessing. Jesus said, "Let the little children come." He didn't say, "force them, scare them, or trick them into the treat of salvation."

- You may also want to have some fun Christian children's music playing on your front porch.

- Happy, non-scary decorations on your lawn or porch can have a positive impact on your neighbors.

- Make certain that your sidewalk and porch are well lit and free of debris.

Ideas for Those Who Want to Do a Little Bit More:

- Set up a mini carnival on your driveway or front lawn. Remember, it's your party. You can do as much or as little as time and finances allow. Here are some things you can do to set up a mini carnival atmosphere.

  ○ Set up one or two simple carnival games such as a beanbag toss or rubber duck race in a washtub.

  ○ Serve hot cider or chocolate to those coming to your house. This can be made on the spot or prepared ahead of time.

  ○ Some people have set up their barbecue and cooked hot dogs for the kids. Be sure to have your cooking area roped off so that children do not get burned on the barbecue. Set up a table with a covering to hold condiments. If you want the dogs to be really fun, add food coloring to your ketchup or mustard. Include nontraditional items for the dogs like chocolate sprinkles, caramel syrup, or peanut butter and jelly.

o Decorate with fun, non-scary decor. Balloons, pumpkins, and other fall items can be displayed. Keep anything dangerous away from the kids.

o Set up a TV and DVD with a fun kids' movie playing. Several chairs or hay bales can be spaced as seating for this.

o Set up a covered table where children can make their own treats. Cookie decorating is probably the easiest make-your-own treat to set up. Sugar cookies can be purchased at a local bakery. (People are less suspicious of store-bought food items.) The children can decorate these with colored frosting, sprinkles, or mini M&Ms.

o Welcome every child as if he/she was Jesus Himself. Some kids will return to your event again and again throughout the evening. Love on them every time they arrive.

o Prepare some treat bags ahead of time. These should include a large portion of candy and a gospel tract.

Things to avoid:

• Clowns or costumed characters in your yard will tend to scare off smaller children. If you must have one of these, make certain that he/she is neat, clean, and attractive, and has a human counterpart. Make sure that he/she allows children to approach him/her rather than the other way around. Clowns and large costumed characters should not invade a child's space.

- Hard-selling the gospel on this night will not endear you to your neighbors. Consider this a drink-of-water kind of ministry. Blessing children and families will bring a return. Gospel tracts, Christian videos, songs, and even puppet shows can be utilized to deliver the gospel message.

- Making this a complicated event will ruin it for you and the kids. Do not stress out over this. You can do as much or as little as time and finances will allow. The point is to have fun helping the children to have fun and to share the love of Jesus with all who come to you.

- Scary costumes, decorations, or entertainment must be avoided. Preschool and elementary children do not need a "hell house" kind of experience. Fun spooky games like "guess what's in the bucket" are acceptable. (This is a game in which several buckets hold things like cooked pasta, Jell-O, or oiled grapes. A towel is thrown over each bucket. Children reach under the towel and guess what's in the bucket.)

- Poorly lit or cluttered walkways. Make sure that when children step onto your property, they can get around without tripping over boxes, bags, or buckets. Lighting with construction lights or household lamps will help children see where they are going and what to avoid.

- Foods that might cause an allergic reaction. We know that most anything could do this, but there are some common foods that rise to the top. Peanuts should not be served in any form. Check with your public school nurse to see what should be avoided in this category.

- Offending the returning child should be avoided. Some kids will want to come back to your "fun" yard after trick-or-treating in the neighborhood. Bless every child with as much love, food, and attention as you can whether they show up once or return five times that night.

- Put away anything that might be deemed dangerous to the health and well-being of children.

Have Fun!

JESUS BLESSES
THE CHILDREN

This is a comparative chart of the Synoptic Gospel presentations of Jesus welcoming the little children.

Matthew 19:13–15	Mark 10:13–16	Luke 18:15–17
Then people brought little children to Jesus for him to place his hands on them and pray for them.	People were bringing little children to Jesus for him to place his hands on them,	People were also bringing babies to Jesus for him to place his hands on them.
But the disciples rebuked them.	but the disciples rebuked them.	When the disciples saw this, they rebuked them.
	When Jesus saw this, he was indignant.	
Jesus said, "Let the little children come to me, and do not hinder them, for the kingdom of heaven belongs to such as these."	He said to them, "Let the little children come to me, and do not hinder them, for the kingdom of God belongs to such as these.	But Jesus called the children to him and said, "Let the little children come to me, and do not hinder them, for the kingdom of God belongs to such as these.

Matthew 19:13–15	Mark 10:13–16	Luke 18:15–17
	Truly I tell you, anyone who will not receive the kingdom of God like a little child will never enter it."	Truly I tell you, anyone who will not receive the kingdom of God like a little child will never enter it."
When he had placed his hands on them, he went on from there.	And he took the children in his arms, placed his hands on them and blessed them.	

FIVE THINGS JESUS WANTS YOU TO SEE IN CHILDREN'S MINISTRY

Introduction

Charles Spurgeon once said, "Children need the gospel, the whole gospel, the unadulterated gospel; they ought to have it, and if they are taught of the Spirit of God they are as capable of receiving it as persons of ripe years."[1] I believe Charles Spurgeon.

Over the years I have studied various aspects of children's ministry and have developed this book to enhance your understanding of this vital ministry in our dying world. George Barna writes, "The world is becoming more complex, but kids maintain the same basic needs as they have for decades: to be trusted, to be loved, to feel safe and to identify a significant purpose in life."[2] I believe that church, and more specifically the Christian family in cooperation with the church, is the God-ordained agency for meeting the needs of children.

In this book, I will show the reader five concepts that need to be in place in order for effective children's ministry to unfold.

---

1 Charles H. Spurgeon, *Come Ye Children* (Pasadena, TX: Pilgrim Publishing, 1975).

2 George Barna, *Transforming Children into Spiritual Champions* (Ventura: Regal Books, 2003).

The five things Jesus wants you to see in children's ministries are: calling, care, communication, cultivation, and cooperation. You will discover that each of these springs from a biblical mandate. Church leadership desires a balanced, growing ministry to boys and girls. The implementation of these five concepts can bring that goal to fruition.

Jesus loves the little children. He always has and always will love them. I believe that the closer a true believer comes to our resurrected Lord, the more that believer will have a love for children. That love, when transferred to service in the church, will do much to bring boys and girls to the Lord. That love, coupled with these five principles, will break down strongholds and release children and families into new life and ministry in Jesus.

Calling

Colossians 1:29 reads, "To this end I strenuously contend with all the energy Christ so powerfully works in me." Like Paul, we each have a calling. This calling translates into compassionate labor for His Kingdom. My calling is to reach, teach, and disciple children. It is a very personal and very real calling. The church is also called to children in a very real and very personal way. Throughout Scripture, God's people are commanded, encouraged, and exhorted to teach the children. In Psalm 78 the writer admonishes God's people to teach the children. Verse 4 reads, "We will not hide them from their descendants; we will tell the next generation the praiseworthy deeds of the Lord, his power, and the wonders he has done." The Psalmist goes on for several more verses, giving good reason for this kind of training. We find in verse 7 the ultimate reason that children need to learn of God. It says, "Then they would put their trust in God."

I find it interesting that this communal calling is encouraged throughout the Old Testament, and that within it we find a Scriptural presupposition concerning children. The Old Testament believer assumed that children could understand and put their trust in God. Jesus reinforced this concept through his teachings in Matthew 19:14, Mark 10:13–16, and Matthew 11:25, where he says, "I praise you, Father, Lord of heaven and earth, because you have hidden these things from the wise and learned, and revealed them to little children."

We cannot ignore the biblical calling to reach and instruct children. One of my students, Jennifer, served as a children's pastor while in college at a local church. One week a little girl named Maria from her church was rushed to the children's hospital. She was having severe headaches and nonstop convulsions. Jen prayed with her Wednesday night crowd for little Maria. Maria was healed at the instant the children's group prayed. Jennifer called me on Thursday morning and said, "Now I know that children's ministries is more than just snack time and puppets." Jennifer had begun to understand the calling.

A church that understands the calling will provide finances, people, and other resources to reach and disciple children. The church must value children because Jesus values children. It is part of my calling as a children's leader to cast the vision of this important ministry into the waters of church normalcy.

Care

When Jesus admonished his followers to "let the children come," he showed godly motivation acted out through human kindness. We must care for the little ones. The act of caring for children comes easily for the children's pastor, for he or she feels a divine empowerment to care for the little ones. The church, however, must be nurtured into caring for the children.

Lois Lebar wrote, "Whereas many adults must be compelled to come to Christ, the children are eager to come if only we adults get out of their way and let them come."[3] We must care enough about the children to get out of their way. We are sometimes so busy dragging, coercing, scaring, or pushing children towards Jesus that our very actions are driving them away. We must let the children come through loving nurture and age-appropriate language and lessons. Charles Spurgeon describes the kind of caring needed to win a child when he says, "Here then is the secret. You must impart to the young your own soul; you must feel as if the ruin of that child would be your own ruin."[4] Let us as a church begin to care for the children as if each little one was our own.

Joe taught our three-year-olds class in Salem, Oregon. He cared for his flock of three-year-olds as a shepherd cares for his flock. Joe had at least five other adult workers by his side each Sunday. Each worker was hand-picked and trained by Joe. In the three years I served at that church, I witnessed grade school, high school, and even college-age people approach Joe for prayer. He had pastored the three-year-olds for seventeen years. He cared so much about his kids that they knew they could come to him anytime for prayer and encouragement. That kind of connection is needed in our fragmented world. Joe's caring attitude was played out in his faithfulness to that class and all who passed through it. Joe was living out what Lawrence Richards wrote about when saying, "Those who care about children will make

---

3   Lois Lebar, *Children in the Bible School* (Old Tappan, NJ: Fleming Revell Company, 1952), 20.

4   Spurgeon, *Come Ye Children*.

a deeper commitment and provide long-term relationships and endless love that make faith community God's unique context for His kind of ministry with boys and girls."[5]

Communication

A great part of our task as children's leaders is to communicate. We communicate the gospel to children, the calling to parents, and the vision to the church. All we do is communication. After about three months in my first children's pastorate, I stormed into my pastor's office. I shouted, "I can't get any work done! People keep interrupting me!" My pastor smiled and calmly said, "Your work *is* people." It is tough to work with people if you lack communication skills.

We communicate the gospel to children. In 1948, Frank Coleman wrote, "No child should be left to grow up in our world of unbelief and flagrant sin without his having heard the gospel with persuasive invitation to believe it and accept its salvation."[6] We must communicate the need for salvation to boys and girls. Communication implies that we understand the child's ability to understand. We take into consideration the needs of the child, his stage of development, and his environment. I cannot preach the gospel the same way to an inner city five-year-old as I do to a rural eleven-year-old. A child who is physically hungry must have that need met before he can comprehend the spiritual significance of Jesus' death on his behalf.

First Thessalonians 2:8 states, "We loved you so much, we were delighted to share with you not only the gospel of God but our lives as well." Children often catch more of what we

---

5 Lawrence Richards, *A Theology of Children's Ministry* (Grand Rapids, MI: Zondervan, 1983).

6 Frank Coleman, *The Romance of Winning Children* (Cleveland, OH: Union Gospel Press, 1948), 9.

live than what we as a church say. The church of today must approach children's work as a life-communication ministry. The sharing of a life will perpetuate the feelings of family, belonging, and importance that a child needs.

We communicate to parents. Postmodern parents need to take a leading role in the Christian education of their children. "Let no Christian parents fall into the delusion that the Sunday school is intended to ease them of their personal duties."[7] Parents are the primary Christian educators of their children. The average children's ministry may have a child under its care two or three hours a week. The impact of a parent during the many hours a child spends at home and en route to school, lessons, or sports is crucial to a child's acceptance of the message presented at church. So we communicate the vision to parents and support them with training and materials to enrich the training of their children in the home. We also provide opportunities for parents to serve their children in the church.

We communicate to the church. I once had a children's pastor complain to me that she could not find any workers in her church. She said, "Nobody cares about this ministry." After evaluating her recruiting strategy, I discovered that nobody knew about her ministry. We must communicate the vision and joy of serving children in as many ways as possible. People do not want to hear about the horrors of serving in the two-year-old class. They want to be part of a ministry that is proactive and on fire for God!

Another point that must be addressed in communication is one of authority. In Matthew 7:28–29 we read, "the crowds were amazed at [Jesus'] teaching, because he taught as one who had authority, and not as their teachers of the law." Our teaching must

---

7   Spurgeon, *Come Ye Children.*

be that of a sensitive authority. It is not acceptable that Sunday school teachers come in half prepared, reading lesson material directly from a quarterly. Children need teachers who live the lessons. We must spend the time necessary in prayer and preparation to become Christlike in our teaching. "Every real teacher's power must come from on high. If you never enter your closet and shut the door, if you never plead at the mercy seat for your child, how can you expect that God will honor you in its conversion?"[8]

Cultivation

"Start children off on the way they should go, and even when they are old they will not turn from it."[9] The kind of training we are directed to be involved in is more than talking and teaching. We must disciple children and their parents in the Christian life. My grandparents raised chickens on their farm sixty-five miles west of Omaha, Nebraska. As children, we nine Gruber boys and girls all pitched in to feed, water, and care for those chickens. When butchering day came, even the youngest participated. We all had a role to fill in this group project. We all had worth. We all had importance. Concepts of responsibility, integrity, and doing our best were cultivated in us through this activity. The chickens we cared for and eventually butchered would help to feed our family through the winter months. Sunday school is a place where children can participate in a similar manner. Children are not butchering chickens. They are discovering the great treasures of God's Word. They are learning basic concepts of responsibility, integrity, and doing their best.

Dr. Billie Davis writes of the importance of learning in a group setting. "After the calling of the disciples, every major

---

8   Spurgeon, *Come Ye Children*, 154.

9   Proverbs 22:6.

incident and discourse includes some mention of them. This indicates their presence is not simply an incidental description of the scene. The disciples had a primary group relationship with Jesus." Jesus demonstrated throughout His ministry the importance of His learners. He set an example in cultivating as He trained His disciples to have a godly worldview.

In the early childhood years we begin the cultivation process with children. Pre-evangelism attitudes, vocabulary, and feelings are developed. Important feelings concerning the Bible, the church, and the family are planted in the hearts and minds of these little ones. Many children's pastors relegate the preschool area to volunteers in favor of elementary ministries that they are more comfortable managing. I want to encourage the reader to study early childhood development. Cultivate relationships with children and their parents beginning in the nursery class.

During my ministry as children's pastor in Bloomington, Minnesota, I spent the last thirty to forty minutes of each Wednesday night serving in the baby nursery. I sang songs, told stories, held babies, and played on the floor. I believe this has had an impact on the children that came through the nursery in those years. A secondary impact was the growth in numbers of workers willing to serve in our nurseries. I believe I was taking the lead in cultivating this ministry. "The Lord Jesus looks with pleasure upon those who feed His lambs, and nurse His babies; for it is not His will that any of these little ones should perish."[10] If we remember that cultivation of a crop in farming is a long-term process, it will help us to grasp the importance of consistent ministry to children throughout the first twelve years of life.

---

10 Spurgeon, *Come Ye Children*, 59.

Cooperation

A couple of years ago, I finished my basement. I enjoy carpentry work, and this large project was a nice diversion from the normal activities of a college professor. I also enjoyed the assistance of more than a dozen college students on this project over a period of several months. They hauled heavy materials and hung sheetrock on the ceiling. They helped me paint and run wiring. I could have struggled alone in finishing this project, but the students now visit my home and proudly point out their contribution to the finished product. My grandfather used to say, "You don't build a house alone." Likewise, the church is a cooperative effort.

A child's spiritual development is a progressive action. Over a period of months and years as the child grows under our ministries, we hope that he/she is led into a genuine relationship with Christ. "If we provide small children frequent opportunities to say, 'yes' to Christ in accordance with their limited comprehension of Him, we shall never err by hindering them from coming to the Savior, nor by being responsible for their making a mere profession before the Spirit has prepared the heart."[11] Lawrence Richards further emphasizes this concept when he writes,

> Ultimately, our assurance of a relationship with God does not come because we remember when we made a verbal commitment, but because we increasingly commit ourselves to live for Him, and discover a growing trust and love. It would be wrong to deny the possibility of childhood conversion. But it would also be wrong to treat response by a child to an evangelistic appeal as an end in itself.[12]

11 Lebar, *Children in the Bible School*, 171.

12 Richards, *A Theology of Children's Ministry*, 375.

Cooperate with other ministries in the church. It only does you harm to walk around mumbling and grumbling about another staff member or a Sunday school teacher who has offended you. Carrying an offense will diminish your effectiveness with the children. I make it a practice to pray for the other pastors and ministries of the church. You can always find some other ministry that gets more money, or better rooms, or greater pulpit announcements. Forget it. We are in this together. You cannot minister effectively if you are mad at the senior pastor. I agree with Jim Wideman when he writes, "I believe you work for the pastor. It's your job to find out what the pastor wants and to deliver it."[13] Children will receive the message you live, and cooperation in the body is paramount to their lifelong survival as believers.

Conclusion

I know that there are many other concepts and principles in children's ministry to be explored. But I cannot neglect the importance of your example. Children watch their teachers. They watch you in and out of the children's church room. They observe your enthusiasm in worship, faithfulness in giving, and reverence at the altars. "As a leader, how you live your life is far more important than where your name appears on an organizational chart."[14] We must live a life of holiness and joy. Children are full of joy and love people who express joy in their living.

It is tough to be around children for very long and not become joyful. I recently preached a children's crusade in a small church in central Pennsylvania. On the first night of the crusade, about forty children were present. When the service concluded

---

13 Jim Wideman, *Children's Ministry Leadership* (Loveland, CO: Group Publishing, 2003).
14 Ibid.

and all were leaving, a little four-year-old girl ran up to me and gave me a great big hug and a smile. I don't remember how joyful I was during the service, but I certainly was full of joy when I left that night.

In this book, I have briefly discussed five things Jesus wants you to "C" in children's ministry. They are calling, care, communication, cultivation, and cooperation. Evaluate your ministries and feed His lambs in each of these areas.

Remember the story of Jairus's daughter. Jesus took the little girl by the hand and said, "Little girl, arise." Taking another human being by the hand is a very personal act. We are in the business of raising children from spiritual death. We are God's hands in this darkened world. As Jesus with flesh on, we take children by the hand and let them come to Christ. I know Jesus wanted you to see that.

LEADING A CHILD TO CHRIST

A Quick Guide

Scriptures: Remember that there are no age limitations attached to any salvation verse. The Bible is not age exclusive. Therefore, any verse that you use in explaining salvation to adults can also be used with children. Here are a few I use.

Matthew 19:14   Romans 3:23

Romans 6:23   1 John 1:8–9

Colossians 2:6–7 John 1:11–12

Acts 16:31

Things to remember:

- ❏ Use kid language and concepts.
    - ○ Always begin at a place of mutual understanding.
- ❏ Keep it simple.
    - ○ Don't be a confusing counselor.
- ❏ Be kind and loving.
- ❏ Don't make assumptions.
    - ○ Why does he want to pray?
    - ○ Presupposition of biblical knowledge.

- ❑ Don't push.
  - ○ Let the child come . . . .
- ❑ Ask questions.
  - ○ Allow the child to discover the answers.
- ❑ Allow the child to ask questions.
- ❑ Encourage the child to pray.
  - ○ Call and response.
  - ○ In his own words.
- ❑ Admit, Ask, Accept.
- ❑ Do not scare the child.
- ❑ After prayer, ask, "Where is Jesus?"
- ❑ Follow up.

PRAYING WITH CHILDREN TO RECEIVE THE HOLY SPIRIT

Children and the Baptism in the Holy Spirit

In Mark 1:8, John the Baptist states, "I baptize you with water, but he will baptize you with the Holy Spirit." Jesus says in Acts 1:5, "For John baptized with water, but in a few days you will be baptized with the Holy Spirit." What is the Baptism in the Holy Spirit? In order to help children understand and receive, I first talk about what this experience is not. Years ago, one of my college professors spoke on five things the Holy Spirit is not. I've expanded that to the following teaching. It has been evident, when teaching this material, that children more easily receive the gift of the Spirit after understanding what the Baptism in the Spirit is and isn't.

The Baptism in the Holy Spirit is:

- **Not the same as salvation.** This is a separate and unique gift following conversion. (Acts 19:1–6)

- **Not for adults only.** This empowerment is for every believer. (Acts 2:39)

- **Not natural.** It is a supernatural experience. A child cannot be taught how to speak in tongues. Jesus is the baptizer. (Luke 3:16; Acts 1:4–8)

- **Not just for Bible times.** This experience is for today. (Acts 2:39)

- **Not an experience where tongues are optional.** Those baptized in the Spirit will receive power and a prayer language. Children take their cues from the adults around them and often pray to receive tongues. Encourage them to pray for more of God's Spirit and power. The tongues will follow. (Acts 1:8; 10:44–47)

- **Not a sign that you have arrived.** The Baptism in the Holy Spirit is a beginning. The content of Acts occurred following Pentecost. The disciples prayed multiple times for more of God's Spirit. (Acts 2:4; 4:31)

- **Not Scary.** God will do nothing scary to a child. I've found that once children overcome the fear of the unknown, it is easy for them to be filled to overflowing with the Spirit. (1 John 4:16–18; 2 Timothy 1:7)

WHEN PRAYING WITH CHILDREN FOR THE BAPTISM IN THE HOLY SPIRIT:

Let them come to Jesus

Praying for this should never be forced, rushed, or confusing. When children express a desire to receive, pray. Jesus said, "Let the children come to me." He did not say, "Drag, coerce, push, force, threaten, or browbeat them to come to me." Sadly, prayer times for and with children have occasionally included just that. I have witnessed people holding children down until they received. At one camp, an adult was shaking a child by the shoulders and demanding that the child receive. I have even heard a well-meaning worker encouraging children to repeat phrases in order to be filled with the Spirit.

I have also experienced the sweet presence of the Holy Spirit filling children to overflowing. In our church, boys and girls use ministry gifts as they pray with other children. I have participated in many prayer services where children have been saved, healed, and delivered at altars.

Prayer time should be a positive experience for children, especially when praying for the Baptism in the Holy Spirit. Workers must be sensitive to God's leading and encourage children to pray one for another. Physical contact should be limited to a hand on the shoulder, head, or back. When appropriate, a hug may be given to a child. Cry with the children. Laugh with them. Above all, enjoy the presence of God with them at the altar.

Encourage boys to pray with boys and girls with girls. In the mid- to upper-elementary ages, more distraction is evident when children pray for those of the opposite sex. Nothing should be allowed to distract children from meeting with God and receiving all that He has for them.

Speak with confident authority. God has placed you as a leader for such a time as this. If you notice anyone—child or adult—doing something that distracts other children or scares them, put a stop to this. People bring their own experiences into prayer times. Some of these can be loud, obnoxious, or just plain weird. Stick with scriptural norms and encourage the outliers to pray with the children in mind.

Encourage every child to spend a little time with Jesus. Children are directed to find a place to pray at their chairs or another designated area. You will be blessed to see children turn and kneel to pray. Prayer time can become a favorite time for children and adults alike.

Speaking with other tongues is the initial physical evidence of the Baptism in the Holy Spirit. Other evidences occurred in Scripture, but speaking in tongues was the normative evidence (Acts 10:44–47). Evidences such as a rushing mighty wind, prophesies, visions, crying, laughing, and tears have occurred during many prayer times over the years. Speaking with other tongues has always been the dynamic proof of God's overflowing power. You will know a child has been filled to overflowing with God's Holy Spirit when that child begins to speak in another tongue. It is the Holy Spirit enabling him to do so.

BASICS FOR BAPTISM IN THE HOLY SPIRIT RESPONSE TIMES

Keep It Positive!

God wants to fill every child to overflowing with His Spirit. Jesus is still in the business of touching and blessing the children. God desires to do more in the lives of children than we can even imagine.

Listen to the Children

Oftentimes, a child will have pressing prayer requests that are more important to her than being Baptized in the Spirit. Listen and pray about those felt needs first. Then pray about this gift.

God Is Willing

Encourage children to ask God for the Holy Spirit. According to Luke 11:13, if earthly fathers know how to give good gifts to their children, how much more will God, our Father in heaven, give the Holy Spirit to those who ask?

Praise Out Loud

Once they have asked God for His Baptism in the Spirit, encourage the children to praise and glorify God aloud. I have never witnessed a child receiving this gift without first praising God out loud in his own native tongue. It isn't known whether the disciples were praising God or not before receiving the Spirit. We do know that they were immediately declaring the wonders of God in their newfound tongues (Acts 2:5–11).

Let Jesus Be the Baptizer

You cannot baptize people of any age in God's Holy Spirit. You can't yell loud enough, shake hard enough, or hype yourself up enough to make God move any faster in a child's life. So relax. Trust that God knows exactly when the child is ready to receive. Be there to encourage and bless. Praise God in the language you know and He will give you a prayer language at just the right time. There is no magic formula for receiving the Baptism in the Holy Spirit. God is not to be boxed in during response times. I've found that He is really good at filling a child to overflowing at the time when that child—body, soul, and spirit—is ready.

Ask

Never tell a child that he has received the Baptism in the Holy Spirit. Ask him what God is doing. Ask him if he is speaking in tongues. If the answer is yes, encourage him to continue. Too many children have left prayer times thinking that they received because an adult misinterpreted their crying or laughing in God's presence. Anyone who has been filled to overflowing with the Spirit can tell you. They will know they have been filled.

He Who Asks, Receives

I often remind children several times during prayer that according to Luke 11:13, those who ask will receive. God will not allow children to be overcome by a fake or counterfeit response. He will give children a prayer language at just the right time. That prayer language may not sound like any they have heard nearby. God is so big that He can give each child his own tongue.

Speak Out in Faith

Encourage children to speak out by faith when the Holy Spirit gives them even a partial word to say. Oftentimes a child will receive a word or two, say the word, and immediately wonder if this is it. I tell kids to speak out whatever God is giving them and believe that He is going to help them.

Let It Flow

Once a child has received the Baptism in the Holy Spirit, encourage him to pray in tongues. Let him know that he can start or stop praying at any time. Further encouragement to now pray for other children should be given. Let every child who has been filled know that this is a prayer language to be used every day.

Love Them

Spend some time encouraging and showing love to boys and girls who have not yet received the Spirit. It is critical that children leaving after extended prayer with no apparent result be encouraged to walk away believing they should continue seeking this experience until it happens (Luke 11:13). Encourage children to walk by faith, knowing that they will be baptized to overflowing at any minute. I have done this many times with great success and awesome testimonies.

Testimonies

- On the island of Tinian, one girl pushed the button on the elevator and she and all of her friends were Baptized in the Spirit and began speaking in tongues.

- A boy in Seattle, Washington, told me that he was walking to the restroom in the middle of the night. As he walked, the boy began praising God. Before he knew it, he was speaking in a heavenly language.

- A girl in one camp prayed every night. It wasn't until she was at home with her mom and dad that God allowed her to be filled to overflowing and pray in tongues. As a result, Mom and Dad were both baptized in the Spirit as the girl laid hands on them.

Let God Guide You

It is important in any prayer service to let God be God. Do not attempt to force a move of God or raise the spiritual level of the altar time by your own strength. Jesus is the Lord of the response time. Let the children come to Him.

I trust you will teach children about, and pray for, the Baptism in the Holy Spirit. Providing children with regular opportunities to enter God's presence and seek more of His Spirit is part of a healthy children's program.

SOURCES
CONSULTED

"The Big 3 of Children's Ministry." Kidzplace.org. http://www. kidzplace.org/site/c.chJKJXOAJlH/b.316999/k.4527/The_ Big_3_of_Childrens_Ministry.htm (accessed June 2, 2008).

Adam Clarke's Commentary. Electronic Database. Copyright © 1996, 2003, 2005, 2006 by Biblesoft, Inc. All rights reserved.

Allen, Leslie C. "2349 (*zakur*)." In *New International Dictionary of Old Testament Theology and Exegesis.* Edited by Willem A. VanGemeren. Grand Rapids: Zondervan, 1997.

Anderson, James W. "Parental influence factor affecting Christian Faith maturity of children through adolescence." Master's thesis, Augsburg College, 2000. http://clicnet.clic.edu/search?/ lThesis+Anderson/lthesis+anderson/-3%2C-1%2C0%2CE/ frameset&FF=lthesis+anderson&4%2C4%2C (Accessed May 31, 2008).

Aquinas, Thomas. *Summa Theologiae,* PC Study Bible formatted electronic database. Copyright © 2003, 2006 Biblesoft, Inc.

———. *Summa Theologica.* "Whether Children Receive Grace and Virtue in Baptism." http://www.ccel. org/ccel/aquinas/summa.TP.iii.TP_Q68.TP_Q68_ A9.html?highlight=children,augustine#highlight (accessed September 29, 2008).

Augustine. "Baptism and the Grace Which it Typifies are open to all, Both Infants and Adults." In *Nicene and Post-Nicene Fathers,* Series 1, Volume 3. PC Study Bible formatted electronic database. Copyright © 2003, 2006 by Biblesoft, Inc. All rights reserved.

Barna, George. *Transforming Children into Spiritual Champions.* Ventura: Regal, 2003.

Barnett, Tommy, Earl Banning, Peter Hohmann, and Jay Hostetler. "Mobilizing a Millennial Generation." *Enrichment* 4, no. 2 (Spring 1999). Assemblies of God, Springfield, MO.

Barrett, Justin L. and Rebekah A. Richert. "Anthropomorphism or Preparedness? Exploring Children's God Concepts." *Review of Religious Research* 44, No. 3 (March 2003): 300–312.

Barton, Keith C. and Linda S. Levstik. "Back When God Was around and Everything: Elementary Children's Understanding of Historical Time," *American Educational Research Journal* 33, no. 2 (Summer 1996): 419–454.

Bastian, Karl. "Leading a Child to Christ." Kidology. org. http://www.kidology.org/zones/zone_post.asp?post_id=93 (accessed June 2, 2008).

Beckwith, Ivy. *Postmodern Children's Ministry.* Grand Rapids: Zondervan Publishing House, 2004.

Berryman, Jerome W. "Children and Christian theology: a new/old genre." *Religious Studies Review* 33, no. 2 (April 2007): 103–111.

Bible Knowledge Commentary/Old Testament. Copyright © 1983, 2000 Cook Communications Ministries.

Bible Knowledge Commentary/New Testament. Copyright © 1983, 2000 Cook Communications Ministries.

Boyd, David John. "The Church's Role in Building the Spiritual Foundation of Children." Master's thesis, Assemblies of God Theological Seminary, 2006.

Brekus, Catherine A. "Children of Wrath, Children of Grace: Jonathan Edwards and the Puritan Culture of Child Rearing." In *The Child in Christian Thought*. Edited by Marcia J. Bunge. Grand Rapids: William Eerdmans Publishing Company, 2001.

Brewster, Dan. "The 4/14 Window, Children, and Missions Strategy." Lecture, Fuller Theological Seminary, 1996.

Bruner, Frank Dale. *Matthew: A Commentary, Volume 2, The Church Book*. Dallas: Word Publishing. 1990.

Buckland, Ron. "Round Table" (Review of *Children Finding faith: Exploring a Child's Response to God*, by Francis Bridger). *Journal of Christian Education* 44, no. 1 (2001).

Cavalletti, Sofia. *The Religious Potential of the Child*. Chicago: Catechesis of the Good Shepherd Publications, 1992.

Charles Spurgeon Biography. http://www.wholesomewords. org/biography/biorpspurgeon.html (accessed September 30, 2008).

Children's Defense Fund Website. http://www.childrensdefense. org/site/PageServer?pagename=research_national_data_ moments (accessed September 5, 2008).

Choun, Robert J. and Michael S. Lawson. *The Complete Handbook for Children's Ministry*. Nashville: Nelson Publishers, 1993.

———. *The Christian Educators' Handbook on Children's Ministry*. Grand Rapids: Baker Book Company, 1998.

Christensen, Randy. *Crucial Concepts in Children's Ministry*. Tulsa: Insight Publications, 2003.

Clark, Robert E., Lin Johnson, and Allyn K. Sloat, eds. *Christian Education, Foundations for The Future*. Chicago, IL: Moody Press, 1991.

Coble, William. "New Testament Passages about Children." In *Children and Conversion*. Edited by Clifford Ingle. Nashville: Broadman Press, 1970.

Coleman, Frank G. *The Romance of Winning Children.* Cleveland: Union Gospel Press, 1948.

Confirmation. Catholic Encyclopedia Online. http://ww.newadvent. org/cathen/04215b.htm (accessed September 29, 2008).

Cox, Julie, Mary Eason, Joyce Hatfield, and Deborah Ritchie. "Hope for the present: equipping kids for the daily battle against sin." *Evangelizing Today's Child* 22:10–12 (Nov 1995).

Crawford, Dan. *The Prayer-Shaped Disciple.* Massachusetts: Hendrickson Publishers, 1999.

Cully, Iris. *Ways to Teach Children.* Philadelphia: Fortress Press, 1965.

Dobbins, Gaines S. *Winning the Children.* Nashville: Broadman Press, 1953.

Dobbins, Richard. *Troubling Questions for Troubling Times.* http://www.drdobbins.com/articles/article. php?article=9&topic=10 (accessed September 6, 2008).

Doherty, Sam. *How to Evangelize Children.* Northern Ireland: CEF Specialized Book Ministry, 2003.

Dollar, Brian. *I Blew It.* Springfield, MO: Influence Resources, 2012.

Dresselhaus, Richard L. *Teaching for Decision.* Springfield: Gospel Publishing House, 1973.

Dunn, Heather, Amber Van Schooneveld, and Ann Marie Rozum. *Children's Ministries in the 21st Century.* Loveland, CO: Group Publishing, 2007.

Edgerly, George, Efraim Espinoza, and Steve Mills. *Focus on Administration: A Handbook for Leaders.* Springfield: Gospel Publishing House, 1993.

Edward Payson Hammond. http://famousamericans.net/ edwardpaysonhammond/ (accessed September 30, 2008).

Elkind, David. *The Hurried Child*. Reading: Addison-Wesley Publishing Company, 1981.

Estep, William R. *The Anabaptist Story*. http://www.anabaptists.org/history/anastory.html (accessed September 29, 2008).

Exegetical Dictionary of the New Testament. © 1990 by William B. Eerdmans Publishing Company. All rights reserved.

Fields, Roger. "A Matter of Life and Death." Cold Water Café. http://www.coldwatercafe.com/re-imagine/Life_and_death.htm (accessed June 2, 2008).

Freeman, Lynda. "No Cookie-Cutter Children's Ministry." *Pulse*. Kidz Matter, 2014.

Grenz, Stanley. *Prayer: A Cry for the Kingdom*. Peabody, MA: Hendrickson Publishers, 1988.

Gruber, Dick. *Focus on Children, A Handbook for Teachers*. Springfield: Gospel Publishing House, 1993.

Hammond, Edward Payson. *The Conversion of Children*. New York: N. Tibbals and Sons, 1878.

Hayes, Edward L. "Establishing Biblical Foundations." In *Christian Education: Foundations for the Future*. Edited by Robert Clark, Lin Johnson, and Allyn Sloat. Chicago: Moody Press, 1991.

———. "Evangelism of Children." *Bibliotheca sacra* 132, no. 527 Jl-S 1975, 250–264.

Heitzenrater, Richard. "John Wesley and Children." In *The Child in Christian Thought*. Edited by Marcia J. Bunge. Grand Rapids: Eerdmans, 2001.

Hendricks, William L. *A Theology for Children*. Nashville: Broadman Press, 1980.

———. "The Age of Accountability." In *Children and Conversion*. Edited by Clifford Ingle. Nashville: Broadman Press, 1970.

Hertel, Bradley R. and Michael J. Donahue. "Parental Influences on God Images among Children: Testing Durkheim's Metaphoric Parallelism," *Journal for the Scientific Study of Religion* 34, no. 2 (June 1995): 186–199.

Honeycutt, Roy. "Children and Conversion." In *Children and Conversion*. Edited by Clifford Ingle. Nashville: Broadman Press, 1970.

Hook, Jennifer. "The role of the church in early childhood faith development." Master's thesis, Concordia University, 2006. http://clicnet.clic.edu/search?/m378.8776+CMe749/ m378.8776+cme749+/1%2C1%2C298%2CE/ frameset&FF=m378.8776+cme749+&252%2C%2C298 (accessed May 31, 2008).

Horn, Cornelia B. "The lives and literary roles of children in advancing conversion to Christianity: hagiography from the Caucasus in late antiquity and the middle ages." *Church History* 76, no. 2 (June 2007): 262–297.

Hunt, Lionel. *Handbook on Child Evangelism*. Chicago: Moody Press, 1960.

———. *Mass Child Evangelism*. Chicago, Illinois: Moody Press, 1951.

Infant Baptism, Age of Accountability, Dedication of Children. http://www.ag.org/top/Beliefs/gendoct_11_accountability. cfm (accessed September 23, 2008).

Ingle, Clifford. *Children and Conversion*. Nashville, Tennessee: Broadman Press, 1970.

IVP Bible Background Commentary: Old Testament. Copyright © 2000 by John H. Walton, Victor H. Matthews and Mark W. Chavalas. Published by InterVarsity Press. All rights reserved.

Jamieson, Fausset, and Brown Commentary. Electronic Database. Copyright © 1997, 2003, 2005, 2006 by Biblesoft, Inc. All rights reserved.

Jones, Edgar. "Forbid them not: Salvation of the Innocents." Voice of Jesus.org. http://www.voiceofjesus.org/salvationhistory1.html (accessed June 2, 2008).

Joy, Donald. "Why Teach Children?" In *Childhood Education in the Church.* Edited by Roy Zuck and Robert Clark. Chicago: Moody Press, 1975.

Keil and Delitzsch Commentary on the Old Testament: New Updated Edition. Electronic Database. Copyright © 1996 by Hendrickson Publishers, Inc. All rights reserved.

Kimmel, Tim. *Grace Based Parenting: Set Your Family Free.* Nashville: Thomas Nelson, 2004. Kindle.

Kummer, Tony. "Childhood Conversion and Age of Accountability." Word Press.com http://tonykummer.word press.com/2005/11/25/childhood-conversion-and-age-of-accountability-part-1-introduction/ (accessed June 2, 2008).

Lebar, Lois E. *Children in the Bible School.* New Jersey: Fleming H. Revell Company, 1952.

Lien, Kathryn. "Children's prayer: a response to God." Master's thesis, University of St. Thomas, 1999. http://clicnet.clic.edu/search?/cLD4834.S568+L546+1999/cld+4834+s568+l546+1999/-3%2C-1%2C0%2CE/frameset&FF=cld+4834+s568+l546+1999&1%2C%2C2 (accessed May 31, 2008).

Marano, Hara Estroff. "Honey, Let's Get Divorced." *Psychology Today.* http://www.psychologytoday.com/articles/pto-19990501-000038.html (accessed September 5, 2008).

Martyr, Justin. *Christian Baptism.* In *Ante-Nicene Fathers* Volume 1. PC Study Bible formatted electronic database by Biblesoft, Inc. Copyright © 2003, 2006.

————. *The Guilt of Exposing Children.* In *Ante-Nicene Fathers* Volume 1, PC Study Bible formatted electronic database by Biblesoft, Inc. Copyright © 2003, 2006.

Matthew Henry's Commentary on the Whole Bible. PC Study Bible Formatted Electronic Database. Copyright © 2006 by Biblesoft, Inc. All Rights reserved.

May, Scottie, Beth Poterski, Catherine Stonehouse, and Linda Cannell. *Children Matter.* Grand Rapids: William Eerdmans Publishing, 2005.

Middleton, Barth and Sally Middleton. "True or false: how to recognize a true decision." *Evangelizing Today's Child* 14:14-15 (January 1987).

Morningstar, Mildred. *Reaching Children.* Chicago: Moody Press, 1944.

Morris, Henry and Martin Clark. "Can small children come to Christ to be saved?" Christian Aswers.net. http://christian answers.net/q-eden/edn-f005.html (accessed June 2, 2008).

Mouw, Richard J. "Baptism and the salvific status of children: an examination of some intra-Reformed debates." *Calvin Theological Journal* 41, no. 2 (November 2006): 238–254.

Neff, David. "Love the Children." *Christianity Today* 50 no. 8 (August 2006): 6.

Nordberg, Robert B. "Developing the idea of God in children." *Religious Education* 66, no. 5 (September-October 1971): 376–379.

Nouwen, Henri. *In the Name of Jesus: Reflections on Christian Leadership.* New York: Crossroad, 1989.

Nucci, Larry and Elliot Turiel. "God's Word, Religious Rules, and Their Relation to Christian and Jewish Children's Concepts of Morality." *Child Development* 64, no. 5 (October 1993): 1475–1491.

Overholtzer, J. Irvin. Child Evangelism Fellowship home page. http://www.cefonline.com/content/view/141/ (accessed June 2, 2008).

Paterson, Thomas. *Jesus and the Children: Winning Children for Christ.* Edited by D.P. Thomson. New York: George Doran Company, 1925.

Poloma, Margaret M. and Brian F. Pendleton. "Religious Experiences, Evangelism, and Institutional Growth within the Assemblies of God." *Journal for the Scientific Study of Religion* 28, no. 4 (December 1989): 415–431.

Razu, John Mohan. "Let them come—let them work: receiving/ using children in a globalised world." *Studies in World Christianity* 12, no. 3 (2006): 249–265.

Rhode, Jason. "Getting Started in Children's Ministry." Children's Ministry Archive, Jason Rhode.com. http://www. childrensministryarchive.com/getting-started-in-childrens-ministry.html (accessed June 2, 2008).

Richards, Lawrence O. *Children's Ministry.* Grand Rapids: Zondervan Publishing, 1983.

Richstatter, Thomas. *Sacraments of Initiation: Sacraments of Invitation.* http://www.americancatholic.org/Newsletters/ CU/ac0301.asp (accessed September 29, 2008).

Roehlkepartain, Jolene. *Children's Ministry That Works! The Basics and Beyond.* Loveland, CO: Group Books, 1991, revised 2002.

Roos, Simone Anne de. "Young children's God concepts: influences of attachment and religious socialization in a family and school context." *Religious Education* 101, no. 1 (Winter 2006): 84–103.

Roth, Mark. *Seeing Your Child's Worth.* 1995. http://www.anabaptists. org/writings/kidworth.html (accessed September 29, 2008).

Sanders, Tommy. "Talking to Children about Salvation." Bgct. org, Texas Baptists. http://www.bgct.org/texasbaptists/ Document.Doc?&id=2054 (accessed June 2, 2008).

Sheets, Dutch. *Intercessory Prayer.* Ventura, California: Regal Books, 1996. Shelley, Bruce. *Church History in Plain Language.* Dallas: Word Publishing, 1982.

Silvoso, Ed. *That None Should Perish.* Ventura, California: Regal Books, 1994.

Smith, Daniel. *How to Lead a Child To Christ.* Chicago: Moody Press, 1987.

Spurgeon, C. H. *Come Ye Children.* Pasadena, Texas: Pilgrim Publications, 1975.

Staal, David. *Leading Kids to Jesus.* Grand Rapids: Zondervan, 2005.

Stonehouse, Catherine. "Children in Wesleyn Thought." In *Children's Spirituality: Christian Perspectives, Research, and Applications.* Edited by Donald Ratcliff. Eugene, OR: Cascade, 2004.

Stortz, Mary Ellen. "Where or When Was Your Servant Innocent? Augustine on Childhood." In *The Child in Christian Thought.* Edited by Marcia J. Bunge. Grand Rapids: William Eerdmans Publishing Company, 2001.

Strohl, Jane. "The Child in Luther's Theology: For What Purpose do We Older Folks Exist, Other Than to Care for the Young?" in *The Child in Christian Thought.* Edited by Marcia J. Bunge. Grand Rapids: William Eerdmans Publishing Company, 2001.

Tertullian. *Of the Persons to Whom, and the Time When, Baptism is to Be Administered. Ante-Nicene Fathers,* Volume 3. PC Study Bible formatted electronic database by Biblesoft, Inc. Copyright © 2003, 2006.

Tesch, Wayne and Diane Tesch. *From Despair to Heir: Reviving the Heart of a Child.* Santa Ana: Royal Family Kid's Camps, 2008.

The Biblical Illustrator. Copyright © 2002, 2003, 2006 Ages Software, Inc. and Biblesoft, Inc.

The Pulpit Commentary. Electronic Database. Copyright © 2001, 2003, 2005, 2006 by Biblesoft, Inc. All rights reserved.

The Table Talk of Martin Luther. Translated by William Hazlitt. http://www.ccel.org/ccel/luther/tabletalk.i.html (accessed September 18, 2008).

Thompson, D.P. *Winning Children for Christ.* New York: George E. Doran Company, 1925.

Wall, John. "When children became people: the birth of childhood in early Christianity." *Interpretation* 60, no. 3 (July 2006): 338–340.

Wamble, Hugh. "Historic Practices Regarding Children." In *Children and Conversion.* Edited by Clifford Ingle. Nashville: Broadman Press, 1970.

Waters, Faith S. "Evangelical Christian churches' opportunity: after school programs for K-6th grade at risk children." Master's thesis, Bethel College, 2003. http://clicnet.clic.edu/search?/m259.22+W329e+2003/m259.22+w329+e++2003/-3%2C-1%2C0%2CE/frameset&FF=m259.22+w329+e++2003&1%2C1%2C1%2C (accessed May 31, 2008).

Widder, Wayne. "Reviewing Historical Foundations." in *Christian Education Foundations for the Future.* Edited by Robert Clark, Lin Johnson, and Allyn Sloat. Chicago: Moody Press, 1991.

Wideman, Jim. "Who Really Matters?" Jim Wideman.com (May 28, 2008). http://www.jimwideman.com/blog/ (accessed June 2, 2008).

———. *Tweetable Leadership.* Murfreesboro, TN: Jim Wideman Ministries, 2015.

Yoder, Gideon. *The Nurture and Evangelism of Children.* Pennsylvania: Herald Press, 1959.

Yust, Karen-Marie. "Theology, Educational Theory, and Children's Faith formation: Findings from the Faith Formation in Children's Ministry Project." *Association of Professors and Researchers in religious Education Proceedings,* Philadelphia, 2002.

ABOUT THE AUTHOR

Dick Gruber, DMin, has been reaching and teaching children and their leaders since the spring of 1975. He has served as a volunteer, children's pastor, speaker, and KidMin consultant. Dr. Gruber has spent the past fifteen years serving as the Professor of Children and Family Studies at the University of Valley Forge. He is a husband, father, grandfather, musician, artist, and writer. Group Publishing named Dr. Gruber as one of the Top 20 Influencers in children's ministry in 2010. Gruber completed his DMin with the Assemblies of God Theological Seminary in 2015.

for more information

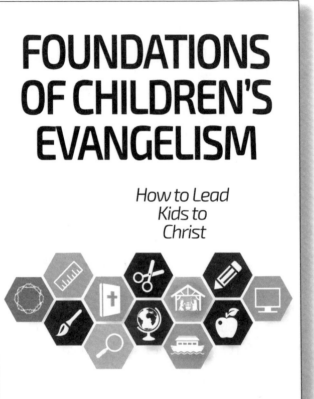

FOUNDATIONS
OF CHILDREN'S
EVANGELISM

*How to Lead
Kids to
Christ*

DICK GRUBER, DMin

FOR MORE INFORMATION about this and other valuable
resources, visit www.myhealthychurch.com.